Care On Call Nursing Agency is working towards achieving the following objectives:

- To be the best
- To make a reasonable profit
- To be responsive and create close working partnerships with clients
- To develop and train our human resource

Being the best implies good service at reasonable prices, in other words value for money. The name CARE ON CALL must be synonymous with value in comparison with others, although we recognise that we shall not always offer the lowest prices. There will be occasions when special terms are negotiated, but setting prices below a certain level can only result in the need for cost reduction and subsequent bad service.

Being the best also implies a strict code of ethical conduct in all business relationships. A reputation for total integrity is vital to growth in this industry. It takes a great deal of time to build up, but can be destroyed by one bad incident.

The CARE ON CALL business relationship starts with the applicant and ends with the client, and there are no circumstances in which a reduction in standards of conduct to either will be tolerated. If a job cannot be handled well, it should not be handled at all.

The following procedures lay down systems and techniques for the efficient operation of the company's service which will enable CARE ON CALL to give optimum value at minimum cost.

However, unless the procedures are applied within the Code of Conduct, their effectiveness will be greatly inhibited.

ADVERTISING FOR STAFF

This procedure deals with placing advertising for staff in newspapers

In this section:

- ■ **Planning advertising**
- ■ **Advertising budgets**
- ■ **Where to advertise**
- ■ **Writing newspaper adverts**
- ■ **Advertising administration**
- ■ **Dealing with advertising responses**

1 Planning Advertising

1.1 Plan advertising according to:

- Staff levels shown by 'staff available' sections
- Customer requirements
- Sales

1.2 Temporary workers are entitled to paid holidays which they can choose to take in summer or at Christmas. Ensure advertising is planned so replacement staff are available to cover for these absences.

1.3 Advertise **EVERY WEEK** except Christmas week.

2 Advertising Budgets

2.1 **DO NOT** go over budget without prior written approval of a manager.

3 Where To Advertise

3.1 Advertise in local papers or the Evening Standard.

3.2 Trade magazine or other media advertising needs a manager's approval

3.3 Decide on the type of advert:

- Display (most expensive)
- Semi-display
- Lineage (least expensive)

3.4 Newspapers quote costs per single column centimetre for display and semi-display adverts or per line for classified or lineage adverts. Request an up-to-date rate card from each paper in your area.

4 Writing Newspaper Adverts

4.1 Decide on the wording of the advert and place with the publisher to meet the print deadline.

4.2 **DO NOT** mix different services in the same advert, like industrial and catering. Advertise each service separately as different candidates will respond to each service.

4.3 **DO NOT** discriminate when wording the advert. Gender specific words, like chambermaid, must be followed by 'M/F' or changed to non-gender specific wording, like 'chamber person.'

4.4 **DO NOT** advertise for someone who speaks 'good English' or any other phrase that could be regarded as discriminatory.

4.5 If lineage advertisements are printed in alphabetical order in a newspaper, ensure that the first word will make the advert appear in the correct place in the listing, for example' Catering staff' will come under 'C'.

4.6 Include '**CARE ON CALL**' in every advert. **DO NOT** abbreviate the name.

4.7 Use the logo in display advertisements.

4.8 If required by a newspaper, add 'agency' to 'Care On Call'.

5 Advertising Administration

5.1 Record the **NET** costing and quote for each advert in the advertising book together with a copy of the wording you submitted.

5.2 Push for discounts from newspapers. The quoted cost is seldom the best price the newspaper will offer.

5.3 Use one page in the advertising book each week, taking Friday as the day the week ends:

- Record the running budget total in bottom left-hand corner

- Record a running total for spending in the bottom right-hand corner

5.4 Keep a copy of the newspaper running the advert, while checking the advert has been included and worded to your specification. If the print-ed advert is incorrect, contact the newspaper and ask for full refund or a discount on future advertising.

5.5 Cut out the advert and stick in book. Record cost of the advertisement **NET** of **VAT**. Study other advertisements in newspaper and repurpose them to improve your adverts.

6 Dealing With Advertising Responses

6.1 Be positive when handling telephone response. Convert good response into interviews.

6.2 Ask all applicants which advertisement they are responding to. Record number of responses next to advertisement. Determine effectiveness of advertisement by calculating unit cost divided by responses.

6.3 Consider quality of responses as well as the number of responses. Large numbers of unsuitable responses are not cost-effective.

6.4 Check the newspaper invoice against the adverts listed in the advertising book and the quoted cost.

6.5 If incorrect, record invoice number and date passed next to advertise-ment. Write 'OK To pay', your initials and your service centre 2 digit prefix and place in payroll drawer for next submission to accounts.

6.6 Chase missing invoices with the newspaper. Ensure that all invoices are received and passed by the close of the financial year (end of March).

6.7 Change advertising copy regularly. **DO NOT** repeat the same wording for more than two weeks in a row.

6.8 Share effective advertising copy with other service managers.

6.9 **DO NOT** place advertisements at Christmas or Easter wishing staff or customers 'Happy Christmas' or 'Season's Greetings'.

6.10 Keep advertising copy for **TWO** years – current year and previous year. Check previous adverts and rerun those with the lowest unit cost.

Documentation

Advertising record – See Resource 1 (Page 151).

PROCEDURE: 0(R)2

WINDOW DISPLAYS

This procedure deals with office window displays

In this section:

- ■ **Window display objectives**
- ■ **Window display notices**
- ■ **Timing window displays**

||||||||||||||||||||||||||||||||||||||||||||||||||||||||||||||||||||||||||||||||||||||||||||||||||||||||||||||||||||||

1 Window Display Objective

1.1 The window display should aim at attracting potential staff.

2 Window Notices

2.1 Order posters and window glue from stationery supplies. **DO NOT** use sticky tape on windows.

2.2 Place general notices in window, for example:

- 'Catering Assistants Required'
- 'Temporary work available now!'

2.3 Notices for specific jobs require a reference number linked to a customer order.

3 Timing Window Displays

3.1 Change the display every week.

3.2 Theme displays with specific times in the year, for example:

- Christmas
- Easter
- Major events, like the World Cup

INTERVIEWING JOB APPLICANTS

This procedure deals with interviewing applicants for jobs

In this section:

- ■ **What applicants should bring to interviews**
- ■ **Interview times and locations**
- ■ **At the interview**
- ■ **Equality and discrimination**
- ■ **After the interview**

IIIIIIIIIIIIIIIIIIIIIIIIIIIIIIIIIIIIIIIIIIIIIIIIIIIIIIIIIIIIIIIIIIIIIIIIIIIIIIIIIIIIIIIIIIIIIIIIIIIIIIIIIIIIIIIIIIIIIIIIIIIIIIII

1 What Applicants Should Bring To Interviews

1.1 Request each applicant to bring to their interview:

- Proof of address

- Proof of identity

- Proof of national insurance number

- Originals of documents proving relevant qualifications, for example, chef's qualifications or a fork-lift licence

- Details of their personal bank or building society account

2 Interview times and locations

2.1 Interview all applicants in person during office hours.

2.2 **DO NOT** restrict interviewing to specific times.

2.3 Conduct interviews in the branch wherever possible. If necessary, conduct interviews at job centres or other suitable locations.

2.4 Do not interview applicants at their homes.

2.5 Do not interview applicants who are aged under 16.

3 At The Interview

3.1 Be polite, friendly and welcoming to each applicant

3.2 Give the applicant a clipboard and pen,

3.3 **DO NOT** keep applicants waiting any longer than necessary.

3.4 **DO NOT** smoke during interviews.

3.5 Conduct interviews without interruptions. Do not interview across messy desks.

3.6 Use a different coloured ink from that used by the applicant.

3.7 Ask the applicant to complete:

- Application card

- Occupational health questionnaire, including night worker assessment

- Equal opportunities questionnaire

- Confidentiality and data protection declaration

3.8 Ask the applicant to answer the skills test on the application card

3.9 Go through the various sections on the application card with the applicant, filling in any gaps and recording relevant information as follows:

- Check proof of identify and record document as seen. Retain a photocopy e.g. passport

- Check proof of address and record document as seen. Retain a photocopy e.g. utility bill

- Check the document giving an entitlement to work and record document as seen. Retain a photocopy, for example, NI number card.

- Identify reasons for leaving each job, record all reasons for any employment gaps, record start and finish dates (month and year) of previous jobs

- Identify and record details of contact, position and telephone number (if known) of referees

- See and check relevant qualifications and record documents as seen. Make and retain a photocopy

3.10 Indicate on the application card any tests which were carried out and mark during interview. Apply pass marks according to service centre or customer requirements.

3.11 Review occupational health questionnaire with applicant.

3.12 In the skills assessment section, record:

- Applicant's skills and experience

- Hours of availability

- Protective clothing owned

- Any work the applicant will not do

- Any other relevant information

- How the applicant came to register with Care On Call, for example, entitlements, word of mouth or walk-in, etc.

3.13 In the case of drivers, record licence details, endorsements and entitlements (See Hiring Drivers 0(I)7)

3.14 In the case of catering staff, if applicant does not have food hygiene certificate, book onto the next available course, record the course date on the application form and issue an "is attending a training course" certificate.

3.15 Request that the applicant completes a P46 and bank account form. Do not complete the bank account form on their behalf. (See Procedure 0(P)12).

3.16 Instruct the applicant to retain P45, but to produce it with their first time sheet.

3.17 Draw the applicant's attention to the terms of engagement.

3.18 Tell all applicants about the Disclosure and Barring Service (DBS) documents. Ensure they answer the relevant question and sign in the correct space on the form.

3.19 Issue Welcome to Care On Call, booklet, relevant guidance leaflets and copy of DBS document.

3.20 Brief applicant with regard to:

- The best time to contact you for work

- Pre-assignment briefings

- How time sheets work and delivery deadline

- Likely pay rates

- Method and time of payment, for example BACS

- Standards and conduct

- Dress requirements

- Qualifying periods and paid leave entitlements

4 Equality and Discrimination

4.1 Hire applicants solely on the basis of ability and merit. Discrimination on any of the following grounds is unlawful:

- Ethnic origin

- Nationality

- Sex

- Colour

- Marital status

- Religion

- Sexual preference

- Race

5 After The Interview

5.1 If an applicant is unsuitable through lack of experience, skills or ability, mark application card '**NPM**' (Not Care On Call Material) and do not offer work.

5.2 Record the details of all applicants in a registration book.

5.3 Record:

- Date

- Name

- Job grade

- Sequential registration number

- Include details of how and where the applicant heard about Care On Call

5.4 Insert the registration number in the space provided on the application card and staple the following documents to the card:

- Occupational Health questionnaire

- Equal opportunities questionnaire

- Bank account form

- P46

- Confidentiality declaration

- Disclosure and Barring Service document

- Terms of Engagement

5.6 Apply for references for all hired applicants by telephone and then follow-up in writing.

Documentation

See Resource 2 (Page 154)

- Application form, including:

— Occupational Health questionnaire

— Bank account form

— Confidentiality declaration/Final statement

- Equal opportunities questionnaire

- Terms of Engagement

- Welcome to Care On Call booklet

EQUAL OPPORTUNITIES

This procedure deals with equal opportunities

In this section:

- **Monitoring equal opportunities**
- **Under-represented groups**

||||||||||||||||||||||||||||||||||||||||||||||||||||||||||||||||||||||||||||||||||||||||||||||||||||||||||||||||||||||||||||||||||||||||||||||||||||

1 Monitoring Equal Opportunities

1.1 Request every applicant to complete an equal opportunities questionnaire as part of the interview process.

1.2 Confirm that all sections have been completed.

1.3 Attach the questionnaire to the application form.

1.4 Conduct monitoring of forms annually.

1.5 Complete monitoring form.

2 Under-Represented Groups

2. Target advertising and recruitment at under-represented groups.

2.1 When targeting under-represented groups, include the following wording in the advertisement: "Applications are particularly invited from (eg disabled applicants) as they are currently under-represented in our workforce."

Documentation

Equal Opportunities Questionnaire (Resource 2b0 Page 162)
Monitoring Form

ENTITLEMENT TO WORK

This procedure deals with a job applicant's right to work in the UK

In this section:

- **Proving entitlement to work**
- **List 1 and List 2 documents**
- **A8 accession countries**
- **A2 accession countries**
- **Overseas student workers**
- **Work permits**

||||||||||||||||||||||||||||||||||||||||||||||||||||||||||||||||||||||||||||||||||||||||||||||||||||||||||||||

1 Proving Entitlement To Work

1.1 All job applicants must produce documentary evidence showing their entitlement to work in the UK.

1.2 The evidence required varies according to their status in the country.

1.3 The Home Office has produced two lists of documents:

1.4 If a person can produce one document from this list they are entitled to work in the UK:

LIST 1 Documents

- Passport showing that the holder is a British citizen

- Passport or other travel document showing that the holder has a right to live in the UK.

- A passport or national identity card showing that the holder is a national of an European Economic Area (EEA) country or Switzerland

- A residence permit issued to an EEA country or Swiss citizen

- A passport or other travel document endorsed to show that the holder can stay indefinitely in the UK, or has no time limit on their stay

- A passport or other travel document endorsed to show that the holder can stay in the UK, and this endorsement allows the holder to do the type of work you are offering.

- An application registration card issued by the Home Office to an asylum seeker stating that the holder is permitted to take a job

||||||||||||||||||||||||||||||||||||||||||||||||||||||||||||||||||||||||||||||||||||||||||||||||||||

European Economic Area (EEA) Countries

Austria	Greece	The Netherlands
Belgium	**Hungary**	Norway
Bulgaria	Iceland	**Poland**
Cyprus	Ireland	Portugal
Czech Republic	Italy	*Romania*
Denmark	**Latvia**	**Slovakia**
Estonia	Liechtenstein	**Slovenia**
Finland	**Lithuania**	Spain
France	Luxembourg	Sweden
Germany	Malta	Switzerland

Countries in **bold** are A8 Accession Countries
Countries in *bold italics* are A2 Accession Countries

||||||||||||||||||||||||||||||||||||||||||||||||||||||||||||||||||||||||||||||||||||||||||||||||||||

- A passport or other document issued by the Home Office which has an endorsement stating the holder has a current right of residence in the UK as the family member of a national from an EEA country or Switzerland who is resident in the UK

1.6 If the job applicant cannot produce a List 1 document, they must produce two documents from the next list in the combinations listed.

List 2 Documents

A document issued by

- A previous employer

- HM Revenue & Customs

- Department for Work and Pensions

- Job Centre Plus

- Employment Service

- Training and Employment Agency (Northern Ireland)

- Northern Ireland Social Security Agency, which includes the National Insurance number of the person named in the document.

AND one of the following:

- A UK birth certificate specifying the names of the holder's parents

- A birth certificate issued in the Channel Islands, Isle of Man or Ireland

- A certificate of registration or naturalisation as a British citizen

- A letter issued by the Home Office, to the holder, which indicates that the person named in it has been granted indefinite leave to enter or remain in the UK

- An immigration status document issued by the Home Office to the holder, endorsed with a UK residence permit, which indicates that the holder has been granted indefinite leave to enter or remain in the UK

- A letter issued by the Home Office, to the holder, which indicates that the person named in it has subsisting leave to enter or remain in the UK and is entitled to take the employment in question in the UK

- An immigration status document issued by the Home Office, to the holder, endorsed with a UK residence permit, which indicates that the holder has been granted limited leave to enter or remain in the UK and is entitled to take the employment in question in the UK

1.7 The second combination also includes work permits, but as work permits are not applicable to temporary work, the information is not relevant.

1.8 Invalid documents include:

- A Construction Industry Scheme (CIS) card

- A temporary National Insurance number

- A National Insurance number ending in a letter from E-Z

2 A8 Accession Countries

2.1 On 1st May 2004, 10 countries joined the European Union and are also became members of the European Economic Area.

Cyprus	Czech Republic
Malta	Estonia
	Hungary
	Latvia
	Lithuania
	Poland
	Slovakia
	Slovenia

2.2 Nationals of these countries are entitled to work in the United Kingdom.

2.3 Only nationals of Cyprus and Malta are entitled to work without restriction, although they still need to prove entitlement. Nationals from the other eight countries must register with the Home Office

2.5 First, check that they are an A8 national by seeing either their:

- Passport

- National identity card (this must show that they are a national or a citizen of the A8 country and not just a resident)

2.6 If they are an A8 national, they need to register for entitlement to work.

2.7 Application forms can be obtained by calling 08705 210224 or by downloading from: www.workingintheuk.gov.uk

2.8 Complete the template letter showing that there is work for them.

2.9 They must complete and send the application form to the Home Office together with any other documents requested and a £70 payment.

2.10 Take a copy of the application form and keep with the registration details.

2.11 The Home Office will register the worker and send you a copy of their registration certificate. Staple the certificate to their application card.

2.12 **DO NOT** offer work until you have received the certificate.

2.13 A8 nationals are exempt from registration if:

- If they have a UK residence permit issued by the Home Office confirming they are an EEA national

- If they have a passport or travel document confirming they have dual nationality with the UK, Switzerland or a non-A8 EEA country

- If they have a passport or travel document endorsing that they are a family member of an EEA or Swiss national

- If they have a passport or travel document containing a valid endorsement showing that they have indefinite or exceptional leave to enter or remain in the UK, or have been granted limited leave to enter or remain in the UK with no restriction on employment

- If they were working legally in the UK on 30 April, 2004 for 12 months without interruption

- If they have worked legally in the UK for 12 months without interruption, falling partly or wholly after 30 April, 2004

- If on 30 April, 2004 they have leave to enter or remain in the UK not subject to any condition restricting their employment

- They are also a citizen of the UK, another EEA state (other than one of the A8 member states)or Switzerland

2.14 The £70 fee is payable to the first time an A8 national registers for work. If they leave their job and go to another one, they must complete a new registration from but do not have to pay again.

3 A2 Accession Countries

3.1 From 1 January 2007, Bulgaria and Romania joined the European Union

3.2 These are known as 'A2 countries' and nationals need authorisation to work in the UK.

3.3 Under the Accession (Immigration and Worker Authorisation) Regulations 2006, employers are required to check whether their A2 workers need to be authorised to work by the Home Office before starting a job.

3.4 Some A2 workers are exempt from authorisation, but if an A2 worker says they are exempt, you still need to ask for documentary evidence.

3.5 A2 nationals who are exempt will be able to apply for a registration certificate, free or charge, to prove their exemption.

3.6 You should ask to see their valid accession worker authorisation document, or a valid exemption registration certificate to ensure that they have the correct entitlement to work.

Template Letter Confirming Offer Of Work

<Branch address>

<Branch telephone number>

Worker Registration Team
Home Office
Walsall Road
Cannock
WS11 0WS

Reference: <Reference>

<date>

Dear Sir

Letter confirming an offer of work

<Worker name> is registering with this employment agency for temporary work.

As a national of an A8 accession country, they are required to register with the Home Office under the Worker Registration Scheme.

They are seeking work as a <job title>.

Yours faithfully,

<Your name>
STAFF CONTROLLER

3.7 If you retain a copy of the document for your records, this will form the basis of the statutory defence to the charge of employing an unauthorised A2 worker.

3.8 Only employ an A2 worker when you have established they can legally work in the UK.

3.8 Accession worker authorisation documents are:

- A document issued before 1 January 2007 that grants leave to enter or remain in the UK and entities that person to work

- A season agricultural work card

- An accession worker card

3.9 An accession worker card is authorisation from the Home Office for the holder to start working for you. The card will also set out any conditions on their employment.

3.10 The Home Office will issue registration certificates to eligible A2 nationals, if satisfied that the applicant is actively seeking employment in the UK and is highly skilled.

3.11 The applicant will then be exempt from the need for work authorisation.

3.12 Any other A2 workers who are not subject to the worker authorisation, may also be issued with a registration certificate that states that they have access to the UK labour market.

3.13 Those A2 nationals who have a registration certificate that does not include a statement saying that they have unconditional access to the UK labour market may apply for an accession worker card after 1 January, 2007, if they can satisfy the Home Office qualifying criteria.

3.14 Check the List 1 or List 2 documents detailed at the start of this section for the following:

- Photographs – does the person look like the photographs on their documents?

- Dates of birth – are the dates consistent with the appearance of the candidate?

- Expiry dates – if the documents have an expiry date, are they still valid?

- Stamps and endorsements – do the passport stamps allow your job applicant to do the type of job you are offering?

- Names – is the same name used on all the documents?

3.15 Photocopy the relevant pages of the document, keep them on file and validate them with the verification stamp.

3.16 The following documents are **NOT** valid as proof of an A2 applicant's entitlement to work.

- A Home Office standard acknowledgement letter (SAL 1 or SAL 2) or Immigration Service letter (IS96W) which states that an asylum seeker can work in the UK.

- A letter issued by the Home Office stating the holder is a British citizen

- A passport describing the holder as a British Dependant Territories citizen which states that they have a connection with Gibraltar

- A bill issued by a financial institution or utility organisation, like a bank statement or gas bill

- A short birth certificate issued in the UK which does not have details of the holder's parents

- Adoption certificates

- A card or certificate issued by HM Revenue & Customs under the Construction Industry Scheme (CIS)

- A driving license issued by the DVLA

3.17 If presented with these documents, advise the applicant to call the Home Office on 0151 237 6375 for information about how they can apply for an application registration card

3.18 EMPLOYING A PERSON WHO IS NOT ENTITLED TO WORK IN THE UK IS AN OFFENCE WHICH CAN INCUR A PENALTY OF UP TO £10,000 PER PERSON, OR TO KNOWINGLY EMPLOY A PERSON WHO IS NOT ENTITLED TO WORK CAN INCUR AN UNLIMITED FINE OR A PRISON SENTENCE OF UP TO TWO YEARS

3.19 SEEING, CHECKING, AND COPYING THE RELEVANT DOCUMENTS ACTS AS A STATUTORY DEFENCE IF PROSECUTED.

3.20 FAILING TO FOLLOW THIS PROCEDURE IS REGARDED AS A DISCI-

PLINARY OFFENCE WHICH MAY BE SUBJECT TO DISMISSAL.

4 National Insurance Numbers

4.1 A National Insurance number is no longer valid as entitlement to work

4.2 Any one with List 1 documents must give a National Insurance number.

4.3 Someone born in the UK is issued with a National Insurance around their 16th birthday. If they do not know the number, they can trace it via their local benefits office.

4.4 Direct an applicant who has recently arrived in the country (eg an A8 Accession National) who does not have a National Insurance Number to the nearest Benefits Agency office (find the address in the phone book)

4.5 They will need to take with them:

- Photographic ID

- Proof that they are actively seeking work – the Welcome to Care On Call booklet may be used or use the standard letter

- Some other form of ID

4.6 The Benefits Agency will take their application and give them a letter acknowledging that they have applied for a NI number

4.7 Check the letter when they return and note the details on the application card. Photocopy the letter, validate with the verification stamp and file.

4.7 Instruct the applicant to produce their NI number as soon as they receive it, and that failure to produce it will lead to work being withdrawn.

4.9 Holders of a List 1 document are entitled to work while they are awaiting their permanent National Insurance number.

4.10 List 2 documents require a permanent National Insurance number and another document. This means that someone who has a List 2 document but does not have a permanent National Insurance number is **NOT ENTITLED TO WORK.**

5 Overseas students

5.1 Students who are not EEA nationals may work provided that:

- The students can provide a letter from their college confirming they are enrolled on a course. The letter must be an original and verified with the signatory. **DO NOT** offer work unless you have seen, checked and taken a copy of this letter. Validate the letter with the verification stamp

- Students cannot work for more than 20 hours a week during term time

5.2 These arrangements do not apply to students on short courses of six months or less who are not entitled to work.

6 Work Permits

6.1 Work permits are obtained by an employer and are only valid for specific employment. They are not available for temporary work. Care On Call cannot and will not apply for work permits for applicants to do temporary work.

6.2 If there are doubts or queries on a document brought in by an applicant and this procedure does not resolve them, call the Employer Helpline on 0845 010 6677.

MONITORING ENTITLEMENT TO WORK

This procedure deals with continuing to check a job applicant has a right to work in the UK

In this section:

- **Reviewing continuing entitlement to work**
- **Monitoring procedures**

||||||||||||||||||||||||||||||||||||||||||||||||||||||||||||||||||||||||||||||||||||||||||||||||||||||||||||||||||||||||||||

1 Reviewing Continuing Entitlement To Work

1.1 Procedure 0(I)3 (See page 17) outlines the entitlement to work procedure that must be followed and the documentary evidence that must be seen before offering an applicant work.

1.2 To ensure our compliance of Section 15 of the Immigration, Asylum and Nationality Act 2006, effective from 29 February, 2008, the following procedure must be followed.

1.3 The procedure ensures that all checks of documentary evidence are recorded and clear evidence of this check is displayed on the front of applicant's registration form to avoid placing applicants who are not entitled to work, whose entitlement has expired or who have not had an annual check.

2 Monitoring Procedures

2.1 Copies of an applicant's documentary evidence of the entitlement to work in the UK in accordance with Procedure 0(I)3 must be taken, stamped as a true and valid copy, signed, dated and the name of the person who checked the documents written clearly on the document for applicants. These copies are retained within the worker's file.

2.2 Following an applicants interview, if they are entitled to work and we intend to find them work, an entitlement to work sticker (See Appendix

A) must be placed in Section G of their registration form in the top right hand side of the shaded area.

2.3 Entitlement to work documents must be checked and re-copied annually for all workers and a new sticker placed on their registration form when they have been checked. Copies of each annual check must be retained in the workers file as proof that when we originally placed the worker they were entitled to work.

2.4 On the sticker write the date checked and expiry date.

2.5 If they have a 'leave to remain for an indefinite period' write INDEF in the expiry date box.

2.6 If they are EEA nationals from a European Economic Area country or a student tick the appropriate box. Remember with students we must see and take evidence of their student status.

2.7 If an entitlement to work expires the worker must not work until new documents have been seen and copied, these being either a new stamp in their passport or an original letter from the Home Office confirming that their right to work is being reviewed. Complete the sticker with the new details. If their renewal application is under review tick the IMM letter box.

2.8 New applicants cannot be given work by showing a Home Office right to work extension letter pending review as their right to work.

2.9 No worker can take a job without an up-to-date sticker.

Entitlement To Work Sticker Template

Date checked:	
Date expires:	
EEA:	
IMM letter:	
Student visa:	
Other	

OCCUPATIONAL HEALTH CHECKS

This procedure deals with monitoring the health of job applicants

In this section:

- **Monitoring job applicant health**
- **Checking health after illness or visits overseas**
- **Keeping health records confidential**

IIIIIIIIIIIIIIIIIIIIIIIIIIIIIIIIIIIIIIIIIIIIIIIIIIIIIIIIIIIIIIIIIIIIIIIIIIIIIIIIIIIIIIIIIIIIIIIIIIIIIIIIIIIIIIIIIIIIIIIIIIIIIIIIIIIIIIIIIII

1 Monitoring Job Applicant Health

1.1 Issue an occupational health questionnaire to each applicant before starting the interview.

1.2 Review questionnaire during interview. Ensure that each section is complete.

1.3 Applicants who answer 'Yes' to having had one or more of the ailments listed below cannot work until their GP states in writing that they are fit to work:

- Diarrhoea
- Typhoid
- Paratyphoid fever
- Bowel/stomach trouble
- Skin – eczema/dermatitis
- Dysentery

1.4 Staple the completed questionnaire to the application card face down.

2 Checking Health After Illness Or Overseas Visits

2.1 When workers are absent due to illness or going abroad, ask them to

---

complete the overseas travel and illness questionnaire.

2.3 Staple the questionnaire face down to the application form.

2.2 Where required by contract:

- Arrange for a doctor to visit the branch.

- Book in required minimum number of staff.

- Receive certificate from doctor on completion of medical.

- Staple certificate to application card, face down and keep confidential.

3 Keeping Records Confidential

3.1 Questionnaires must be kept confidential, so do not discuss the contents with third parties.

Documentation

- Occupational Health questionnaire

- Overseas travel & illness questionnaire

- Doctor's certificate

REHABILITATION OF OFFENDERS

This procedure deals with job applicants with criminal convictions

In this section:

- **Explaining spent conviction**
- **Rehabilitation periods for offenders**

1 Explaining Spent Convictions

1.1 Under the Rehabilitation of Offenders Act 1974, someone who has had a conviction for criminal offence may, with some exceptions, may ignore the offence after a certain period of time.

1.2 The conviction is 'spent' if the individual does not commit another serious offence within the time limit.

1.3 However, the Rehabilitation of Offenders Act 1974 (Exceptions) Order 1975 (SI 1975 No. 1023 as amended) provides that in certain circumstances the Act shall not apply.

1.4 Some workers exempt from the law include:

- Dental workers
- Nurses
- Midwife
- People working with the elderly, the sick, or those with disabilities
- People working with children

1.5 All workers may at some stage work in one of these groups, so we require everyone to make and sign the rehabilitation of offenders declaration on the terms of engagement at interview.

1.6 The rehabilitation period runs from the date of sentencing, while all suspended sentences are treated as if they had been put into effect.

Documentation

Terms of Engagement Declaration – Resource 2c) (Page 164)

|||||||||||||||||||||||||||||||||||||||||||||||||||||||||||||||||||||||||||||||||||||||||||||||||||||||||||||||||||||||||||||||||||||||||||||||||||||||||||||||||

Rehabilitation Periods for Offenders

Sentence	Rehabilitation period	
	Adults (aged 18 or over on conviction)	Young people (aged under 18 on conviction
Imprisonment or detention in a young offender institution for more than 30 months	Never spent	
Imprisonment or detention in a young offender institution for more than 6 months but less than 30 months	10 years	5 years
Imprisonment up to 6 months	7 years	3 years 6 months
Fine	5 years	2 years 6 months
Community sentence	5 years	2 years 6 months
Conditional discharge	Term of order or 12 months, whichever is most	
Absolute discharge	6 months	
Conditional discharge	3 months	
Conditional caution, reprimand, final warning	Spent immediately	

Sentences with variable rehabilitation periods:

Compensation order	On discharge of the order	
Supervision order	N\A	Term of order or 12 months, whichever is most
Bind over	Term of order or 12 months, whichever is most	
Attendance Centre order	12 months after the order expires	

VER: 1 26/04/2013

Sentence	Rehabilitation period	
	Adults (aged 18 or over on conviction)	Young people (aged under 18 on conviction
Hospital order	Five years or two years after order expires, whichever is most	

Rehabilitation periods for members HM Services

Cashiering, discharge with ignominy or dismissed with disgrace from HM Services	10 years	
Dismissal from HM Services	7 years	
Detention resulting from conviction in HM Services disciplinary proceedings	5 years	

|||||||||||||||||||||||||||||||||||||||||||||||||||||||||||||||||||||||||||||||||||||||||||||||||||||||||||||||||||||

OBTAINING REFERENCES

This procedure deals with referencing job applicants

In this section:

- **Who needs a reference**
- **How to check references**
- **Reference administration**

1 Who Needs A Reference?

1.1 Reference all hired applicants. **DO NOT** ask them to bring references when they come for interview.

1.3 **KEEP** copies of references applicants bring, but verify by telephoning the referee.

2 How To Check References

2.1 Check addresses for previous employers for sending written references r

2.2 Check references initially by telephone

2.3 Identify the name and title of the person you are speaking to.

2.4 **DON'T** just ask for the name the applicant has given you.

2.5 Ask whether the applicant was:

- Honest
- Reliable
- A good time keeper
- Capable of the work

Confirm:

- Start and finish dates
- Reasons for leaving
- Whether they would be re-employed

2.6 Ask for any other comments.

2.7 Record comments on the card, with your initials and the date.

3 Reference Administration

3.1 Sent out written reference request. Include a reply paid envelope. Indicate your branch name.

3.2 Record on the application card the date the reference was sent.

3.3 When the reference is returned, check the comments

3.4 **DO NOT** use applicants if the referee's comments are unsatisfactory.

3.5 Staple the reference to the application card.

3.6 Telephone companies to chase delayed references.

3.7 Different customers have different requirements in terms of the number or type of reference taken. Comply with these requirements.

3.8 Establish one reference per applicant, initially by telephone but confirmed in writing, as the standard.

3.9 **Supplying a driver without a satisfactory written reference covering driving work is a disciplinary offence which may lead to dismissal.**

3.10 Respond to temporary staff reference requests accurately and quickly.

3.11 Send reference requests on Care On Call permanent employees to the personnel department at head office.

Documents

- Reference request – See Resource 2a) (Page...)

VER: 1 26/04/2013

HIRING DRIVERS

This procedure deals with referencing driving job applicants

In this section:

- ■ Interviewing driving job applicants
- ■ Reviewing driving licences
- ■ Endorsements
- ■ Vehicle categories
- ■ Driving licence administration

||||||||||||||||||||||||||||||||||||||||||||||||||||||||||||||||||||||||||||||||||||||||||||||||||||||||||||||||||||||||||||

1 Interviewing driving job applicants

1.1 **ONLY** recruit drivers who have previously had a full time driving job.

1.2 Require all driver applicants to produce a full current, British driving licence at interview. Non British driving licences are not acceptable.

1.3 **DO NOT** interview drivers who do not have their licence with them.

1.4 New licences or licence renewals are now issued as a photocard containing brief personal details of the driver with an accompanying paper slip. This accompanying slip must also be produced by driver applicants.

1.5 **DO NOT** interview driver applicants who only have the photo-card.

1.6 **ALL** drivers must be 21 or over

2 Reviewing driving licences

2.1 Record the following information from the driving licence to the application card:

- Licence number

- Driver number. The driver number is a code for the date of birth eg 506223 is 22/6/53

- If the licence is for a female the second digit has a five added eg the number will either be a five or six.

- Issue date

- Expiry date

2.2 A licence with C or C&E entitlement is valid for five years.

3 Endorsements

3.1 Only hire drivers with no endorsements or a maximum of six penalty points. **DO NOT HIRE** drivers with drink or drugs (any DR code), careless driving (any CD code) or dangerous driving (any DD code) convictions.

4 Vehicle Categories

4.1 Modern licences have a picture as well as a description of the vehicle the holder can drive.

4.2 Category codes are as follows:

- B - Car up to 3,500kg or with less than eight seats

- C1 - Goods vehicle 3,500kg -7,500kg.

- C - Goods vehicle more than 3,500kg.

- D1 - Passenger vehicle with more than eight but less than 16 seats.

- D - Passenger vehicle with more than eight seats.

- C1&E - Lorries between 3,500kg and 7,500 kg towing a trailer over 750kg – with a total weight of not more than 8,250kg.

- C&E - Articulated lorries or large lorries over 3,500kg towing a single axle trailer over 5,000 kg or any other trailer over 750 kg.

- D1&E - Buses with between 9-16 seats NOT used for hire or reward, towing a trailer over 750 kg.

- D&E - Combination of buses in category D and a single axle trailer over 5,000kg or any other trailer over 750 kg.

VER: 1 26/04/2013

4.3 The entitlements are indicated by a letter in the third column on a licence, next to the particular type of vehicle.

4.4 Note category restriction indicated by a number in the fourth column

4.5 The most important restrictions are:

- Not for hire-reward

- Drawbar trailers only

- Automatic transmission only

5 Driving Licence Administration

5.1 If the licence address is different from the applicant's current address, record the licence address and inform the applicant that they must get their licence address changed.

5.2 Check:

- The signature on licence against signature on application card.

- The date of birth on application card against that on the licence and driver number.

- If driver has photocard licence, check the photograph matches the driver

- Employment history with specific dates and note reasons for gaps.

5.3 Copy licence and staple to application card.

5.4 Ask all drivers to complete the driver questionnaire.

5.5 Conduct a skills assessment using driver's check-list.

5.6 Take photograph if driver does not bring in photographs.

5.7 Classify drivers as:

- 7.5 ton - if they have C1 entitlement

- LGV - if they have C entitlement

- AGV - if they have C & E entitlement

- PCV - if they have D entitlement

VER: 1 26/04/2013

5.8 Check references by telephone and confirm in writing with the driver reference request form.

5.12 Check licences every six months for endorsements.

Documentation

- Driver's questionnaire
- Driver's checklist
- Driver's reference request

APPLICANT TESTING

This procedure deals with skills tests for job applicants

In this section:

- **Skills Arena Testing**
- **Manual Skills Testing**

|||||||||||||||||||||||||||||||||||||||||||||||||||||||||||||||||||||||||||||||||||||||||||||||||||||||||||||||||||||||||||||||||||||

1 Skills Arena Testing

1.1 Test applicants for commercial work using Skills Arena (where available) and/or manual systems

1.2 Use Skills Arena for:

- Knowledge and understanding of programs eg Word, Excel, Power-Point

- Speed and accuracy in word processing (typing)

- Data entry – numeric and alphanumeric

1.3 Explain the skills test to the applicant and define test requirements.

1.4 Allow applicant to familiarise themselves with the equipment.

1.5 **DO NOT** interrupt applicant during completion of test.

1.6 Staple resulting print out to application card.

2 Manual Skills Testing

2.1 Use manual systems for:

- Spelling

- Arithmetic
- Punctuation
- Filing

2.2 Request applicant to record answers on reverse of application card.

2.3 Mark the test during the interview.

2.4 Record which test was completed.

2.5 Apply pass marks according to customer requirements.

2.6 Do not apply all tests to each applicant. Only apply relevant tests or those required by customers.

Documentation

Manual tests available:

- Spelling
- Arithmetic
- Punctuation
- Filing

POLICE DISCLOSURE AND BARRING CHECKS

This procedure deals with checking police records

In this section:

- ■ **Disclosure and Barring Service overview**
- ■ **Orders needing DBS and POVA checks**
- ■ **DBS application procedure**
- ■ **Sending off completed DBS applications**
- ■ **Dealing with DBS disclosure information**
- ■ **Disclosures from other employers**

1 Disclosure And Barring Service Overview

1.1 The Disclosure and Barring Service (DBS) is the organisation that checks whether applicants have a police record. These checks are called 'disclosures'.

1.2 Disclosure checks are to identify job candidate who may be unsuitable for certain work, especially involving children or vulnerable adults.

1.3 There are two levels of disclosure relating to the check the police carry out:

- Standard

- Enhanced

1.4 **The default disclosure for Care On Call Applicants is enhanced disclosure**

1.6 See appendix A for an explanation of the disclosures and examples of which posts are eligible for which level.

1.7 Requests for disclosure must be countersigned by registered signatories who have passed a DBS check. Care On Call is registered with the DBS, and has a number of staff who can countersign applications for disclosure.

1.8 The rules for accessing DBS are strict. Failure to comply could lead to the company losing registration.

1.9 Failing to comply with the procedures would be regarded as a disciplinary matter which could result in dismissal.

2 Orders Needing DBS and POVA Checks

2.1 This section relates to receiving an order from client for a job which requires a POVA check or a DBS check with a POVA check.

2.2 Record the requirement on a work order in ETQA section.

2.3 Select a temporary worker for who has a D-ENH sticker on their card.

2.4 Check the date that the DBS disclosure was issued.

2.5 If the disclosure was issued after July 26, 2004, complete the template letter (appendix B) and fax to client.

2.6 If the disclosure was issued before July 26, 2004, complete template letter (appendix C) and fax to the client

3 DBS Application Procedure

3.1 When an applicant first calls about work needing a disclosure, tell them they need a disclosure and that they must apply through Care On Call.

3.2 Tell them about the documents that they will need to bring in to confirm their identity when applying for a disclosure - See appendix E for a list of suitable identification

3.3 Only hired applicants and are seeking work needing a disclosure should make an application.

3.4 If the applicant wants further information about the DBS process, show them 'Guidance for Disclosure Applicants.' - See appendix B

3.5 All hired applicants must sign the statement on the DBS document regarding criminal convictions. No applicant can be hired without signing the declaration - See appendix C.

3.6 See appendix D for the Code of Practice (referred to in appendix C).

3.7 Having a criminal conviction does not prevent a person from working, but they **MUST** declare all convictions, including those which might be regarded as spent

3.8 There are two ways of obtaining a disclosure:

- The applicant telephones the DBS to request a disclosure application. **Temporary staff cannot do this**.

- The applicant is issued a disclosure form by Care On Call. Application forms are numbered. Do not waste them.

3.9 The application form must be completed in **BLOCK CAPITALS** using **BLACK INK.** Forms are scanned and the information must be kept within the boxes. If an applicant makes a mistake, cross out the error and insert and initial the correct information alongside.

3.10 If an applicant does not have the required ID with them, they will need to return with the documents.

3.11 Under no circumstances may they take the application form with them. This is to prevent fraud.

3.12 Interviewers must check sections A to E of the form are completed.

3.13 Check the applicant's ID documents for authenticity.

3.14 Take photocopies of the ID documents to keep on file. Mark the photocopies with the verification stamp. Check that sections A and B match the copied documents.

3.15 Enhanced Disclosure costs £36. Applicants must pay the fee, Payment by postal order or cheque is preferred. Cheques and Postal Orders should be payable to Care On Call.

3.16 Issue a DBS receipt and give the money to the petty cash box key holder and the DBS application to the counter-signatory.

3.17 The counter-signatory must complete and sign Section Y.

3.18 The counter-signatory is signing to confirm that the relevant identity checks have been made on the applicant.

3.19 All applicants must be checked against the Independent Safeguarding Authority (ISA) register and counter-signatories must mark boxes 67 in Section X for this.

3.20 See appendix H for guidance for counter-signatories on completing Sections W, X, Y.

3.21 Counter-signatories are responsible for ensuring DBS applications they counter sign are free from errors and that all required checks have been completed

3.22 **Disciplinary action will be taken against counter-signatories who regularly submit incorrect or incomplete disclosure forms.**

4 Sending Off Completed DBS Applications

4.1 Once the DBS forms are counter-signed, the counter-signatory enters the DBS application details into the DBS register.

4.2 Once counter-signed, send the application form, plus payment to the Field Staff Support Department (FSSD) at head office.

4.3 Indicate the service desk name and job analysis number on the envelope.

4.4 Do not send an application form without payment attached.

4.5 Send forms by internal mail. If payment is in cash, put the money in an envelope, staple shut and initial across the flap covering the seal.

4.6 Complete a separate form indicating how many forms are in the bundle, how much money is inside, how the forms were delivered to FSSD and the names of the applicants, along with details of how they paid.

4.7 Envelopes for FSSD taken with payroll must be taped with all the payroll envelopes in a bundle for delivery.

4.8 Separate envelopes should be handed to a senior manager and not left in reception or the accounts department. See Appendix J for a copy form.

4.9 The day after sending forms and payment, confirm receipt with FSSD.

4.10 The person who completed Appendix J should confirm all forms and payment have been received by FSSD.

4.11 If the person who completed Appendix J is absent, someone else from the branch team **MUST** carry out the check.

4.12 FSSD will collate forms and send to the DBS.

4.13 Once the DBS has completed its checks, a disclosure is sent to FSSD.

4.14 If there is a query on a disclosure application, the DBS will contact the counter-signatory direct.

4.15 FSSD will log details and send the disclosure to the branch in an envelope marked 'Private & Confidential – FSSD info' for attention of the team leader.

4.16 Attach a DBS sticker to the applicant's card with the enhanced disclosure's issue and expiry dates.

4.17 Enter the date the DBS disclosure was issued and the expiry date, which is one year less one day from the date when the disclosure was issued.

4.18 Complete the DBS register confirming receipt date.

4.19 Rechecking disclosure must be completed before the expiry date. See Procedure O (I) 9 b.

4.20 When the new DBS disclosure is received, shred the previous form.

5 Dealing With DBS Disclosure Information

5.1 If the disclosure shows convictions, check whether the applicant admitted them on original DBS declaration.

5.2 Applicants did not declare convictions are making a false statement. NPM and do not offer any work.

5.3 Applicants who declared a conviction like a motoring offence, but do not admit other convictions revealed in the disclosure are also making a false statement. NPM and do not offer any work.

5.4 Applicants who have any of the following, even if declared, may not work in any job needing a disclosure:

- Unspent offences against the person, like assault or murder
- Unspent or spent sexual offences
- Unspent or spent drugs offences
- Entry on the ISA register restrictions
- Entry on the Sex Offenders Register.

5.5 See Procedure O(I)5 on Rehabilitation of Offenders Act for an explanation of timescales regarding spent offences

5.6 Applicants banned from working with people under 18 - for instance if they are listed on the ISA Register or the Protection of Vulnerable Adults (POVA) list, commit an offence applying for a job that involves working with vulnerable people.

5.7 Contact Care On Call Department for advice on how to proceed if you receive such an application.

5.8 Applicants who have declared any of the following offences may work in a needing disclosure if the client agrees in writing:

- Spent offences against the person
- Unspent or spent offences relating drugs
- Spent offences relating to theft or dishonesty
- Unspent or spent driving offences

5.9 Applicants who have declared spent offences may work in any role not needing disclosure.

5.9 See Procedure O(I)5 on the Rehabilitation of Offenders Act for information about spent offences.

5.10 File disclosures in a lockable cabinet, either in the applicant's personal file or in an alphabetical index.

6 Disclosures From Other Employers

6.1 If the applicant brings a disclosure applied for by Care On Call, then it is valid for one year from the date of issue.

6.2 If the person has any absence of 12 weeks or more, they must re-register, which includes applying for a new DBS disclosure and POVA check

6.3 The disclosure register should show:

- Service desk number

- Service desk name

- Name of applicant

- Application form number

- Date disclosure form submitted to FSSD

- Date disclosure result received

- The disclosure result - like at D–ENH sticker

- Date disclosure valid from

6.4 These procedures are subject to audit.

6.5 FAILURE TO FOLLOW THESE PROCEDURES IS A DISCIPLINARY MATTER WHICH MAY LEAD TO DISMISSAL.

VER: 1 26/04/2013

PROTECTING VULNERABLE ADULTS

This procedure deals with skills tests for job applicants

In this section:

- ■ **The Protection of Vulnerable Adults List**
- ■ **Disclosure and Barring Service checks**
- ■ **Referring POVA misconduct**
- ■ **Guidance on access to vulnerable adults**

||||||||||||||||||||||||||||||||||||||||||||||||||||||||||||||||||||||||||||||||||||||||||||||||||||||||||||||||||||

1 The Protection of Vulnerable Adults List

1.1 The Protection of Vulnerable Adults (POVA) List was established by the Care Standards Act 2000 as a list of people who have proved themselves unsuitable to work with vulnerable adults.

1.2 Every applicant seeking a position which gives access to vulnerable adults must be checked against the list before they start their job.

See Page XX for guidance on access to vulnerable adults.

1.3 The list is managed by the Disclosure and Barring Service (DBS).

1.4 The job applicant consents to a check by placing a cross in the box in Section Y of the disclosure application form marked 'the position involves regular contact with vulnerable adults'.

2 Disclosure and Barring Service Checks

2.1 Staff who worked with Care On Call before July 26, 2004 who already have a DBS disclosure do not need checking against the POVA list.

2.2 However a POVA check is only valid for 12 months, so staff who work with vulnerable adults must complete a new DBS disclosure every year..

VER: 1 26/04/2013

2.3 A DBS disclosure is regarded as valid for 12 months, except if the person is absent for four consecutive weeks or more, other than for holidays, certified sickness, certified maternity absence or certified jury service.

2.4 Clients who want staff to work with vulnerable adults will require written confirmation that the applicant has been checked against the POVA list. See Page xx for the template letter confirming a POVA check

2.5 An applicant who was employed prior to 26 July, 2004, does not need to have a POVA check until their 12-month employment anniversary. See Page XX for the template letter confirming no POVA check is currently due

2.6 It is a criminal offence for anyone named on the POVA list to knowingly take or apply for a job which involves contact with vulnerable adults. Any applicant whose DBS disclosure shows that they appear on the list will be reported to the police.

2.7 A DBS dsclosure with a POVA check is **NOT PORTABLE** from one company or agency to another. The only exceptions are nursery nurses or nursery assistants whose DBS disclosure is regarded as portable, but they must not work with access to vulnerable adults. See Procedure O(I)9 on Page XX

2.8 Applicants who come with a DBS disclosure from another company must apply for new disclosure and POVA checks.

3 Referring POVA Misconduct

3.1 Care On Call is obliged to someone guilty of misconduct which harmed or placed a vulnerable adult at risk of harm.

3.2 Examples of misconduct include:

- Physical or sexual abuse

- Theft or fraud

- Wilful neglect

- Assisting another person to perform the above acts

- Any other reason any reasonable organisation would deem appropriate

- Falsification of records designed to cover up any of the above acts

3.3 The decision to refer a care worker to the list is made by a director of the company,

3.4 No one will be referred to the list until all stages of the disciplinary process are exhausted.

3.5 If a care worker is alleged to have committed any of the above acts, inform the personnel director in writing as soon as possible.

3.6 The personnel director will investigate and contact all involved parties.

3.7 The worker will be informed if their details are referred to the POVA list.

3.8 The following items of information must be included if a referral is made:

- Full name
- Date of birth
- National Insurance number
- Last known address
- Confirmation the person was a carer at the time of the misconduct
- Full details of the alleged misconduct
- Details of any investigations carried out, including copies of relevant papers, including statements, interview notes, minutes of meetings and details of disciplinary procedures
- Action taken eg has the person been suspended or dismissed ?
- Information on police involvement
- Details of proposed further action eg dates for disciplinary hearings
- Any other information relevant to the alleged misconduct

3.9 Referral information should be sent in via recorded delivery to:

The Manager
Protection of Vulnerable Adults List
Department of Education & Skills
Room 134
Wellington House
133-155 Waterloo Road
London SE1 8UG

VER: 1 26/04/2013

3.10 The Secretary of State will decide whether it is appropriate for a person to be provisionally included on the list and will invite both the person and the provider to make observations before making a final decision.

3.11 Where a person has been referred to the list, all documents and files concerning that person are to be sent to head office for storage.

3.12 Care On Call will breach of the care standards regulations if failing to comply with the POVA requirements.

3.13 Any failure to comply with the requirements of this procedure will be regarded as a disciplinary offence. See Appendix D for the procedure on filing orders which require a DBS disclosure with a POVA check.

3.14 A nursery nurse or nursery assistant DBS check is portable, but they may not work with vulnerable adults.

4 Guidance on Access to Vulnerable Adults

4.1 A vulnerable adult is an adult staying in a care home and receiving nursing or personal care or an adult living in their own home receiving personal care from a care agency.

4.3 A person has access to a vulnerable adult if their job gives them such access. Note - that it does not hinge on their job title or job description, the nature of their duties.

4.4 Just because a person works in a care home does not mean that they have access to vulnerable adults.

4.5 POVA guidance issued by the government gives the following examples:

4.6 Example 1

A care home administrator,helps at meal times every day to ensure that severely or frail disabled residents make their way to the dining room and are assisted in eating their food. It is likely that this would be considered "regular contact" with the result that a POVA check will be necessary.

4.7 Example 2:

An administrator who works in the care home's general office has fleeting contact with residents on arriving and leaving the premises, and only sees residents when they occasionally come to the office looking for the manager for information.

It is unlikely that this would constitute regular contact and a POVA check would not be necessary'.

4.8 When taking an order from a client for do not automatically assume that a DBS disclosure with a POVA check is required.

Template Letter: POVA Check Confirmation

To: <name and address>

Reference: <reference>

Date: <Date>

Dear <Name>

This is to confirm that <worker's name> has been checked against the Protection of Vulnerable Adults (POVA) list as part of their DBS disclosure. This check has been conducted within the 12 months preceding today's date.

Yours faithfully,

<Name>
<Position>

Template Letter: No POVA Check Confirmation

To: <name and address>

Reference: <reference>

Date: <Date>

Dear <Name>

<worker's name> was employed by this agency prior to <date> and, in accordance with guidance issued by the Department of Health, is not required to be checked against the Protection of Vulnerable Adults (POVA) list, until their 12-month anniversary of employment.

Yours faithfully,

<Name>
<Position>

DBS CASH HANDLING

This procedure deals with managing cash held for DBS checks

In this section:

- **Handling DBS cash from candidates**
- **Missing DBS information**

1 Handling DBS cash from candidates

1.1 Disclosure and Barring Service forms can only be processed when payment of £36 is received in cash or cheque. Cheques are preferable.

1.2 On receiving payment, issue a receipt from the DBS receipt book.

1.3 The applicant and the receiver must both sign and date the receipt and the DBS form number should be written in the number section. Issue the bottom of the receipt to the applicant.

1.4 Only issue receipts from your allocated DBS receipt book

1.5 On receiving payment. the DBS application and he payment must be handed to the team leader or the person with the key to the cash box. Attach the top copy of the receipt.

2 Missing DBS information

2.1 If information is missing from the DBS form, the team leader retains the documentation and payment. Put both in a lockable filing cabinet and the cash in a lockable cash box.

2.2 If the missing information is not forthcoming or the applicant leaves before the DBS application is submitted, refund their payment and issue a receipt to confirm this.

VER: 1 26/04/2013

2.3 If the branch holds a large amount of cash for unprocessed DBS applications, pay the money into the company bank account or send to head office to bank DBS processing or a reimbursement. Any cash forwarded to head office or paid into the bank must be recorded, with details kept in the cash box.

2.4 Team leaders or the cash box key holder must balance the cash held against DBS applications pending and receipts issued every month, or if there is a cash box handover.

2.5 Highlight any discrepancies to your operations manager.

2.6 Anyone mismanaging DBS application cash or failing to follow these procedures will be subject to disciplinary proceedings that could result in dismissal.

Template Letter: DBS Renewal Reminder

To: <name and address>

Reference: <reference>

Date: <Date>

Dear <Name>

Your enhanced Disclosure and Barring Service (DBS) disclosure is due to expire on <date>. So Care On Call can continue to offer you work at the places you are accustomed to, you must come to the office to apply for a new DBS disclosure.

Please remember to bring your identity documents and payment of £<amount> to complete the application.

Feel free to call if you can't remember the documents you need to bring in.

Thank you in advance for your co-operation.

Yours sincerely,

<Name>
<Position>

SKILLS TESTS

This procedure deals with managing cash held for DBS checks

In this section:

- **Conducting a skills test**
- **Available skills tests**

||||||||||||||||||||||||||||||||||||||||||||||||||||||||||||||||||||||||||||||||||||||||||||||||||||||||||||||||||||||||||||

1 Conducting a skills test

1.1 Issue skills test to applicant with application card.

1.2 Request applicant to write answers on the application card in the space provided.

1.3 Mark test with applicant during the interview. Indicate on application card which test was completed.

1.4 Establish pass mark according to customer or branch requirements

1.5 Use test score to assist in deciding applicant's suitability.

2 Available skills tests

2.1 Skills tests available:

- Food hygiene (use for kitchen porters)

- Catering assistants

- Domestics and laundry staff

- Chambermaids

- Waiting staff

- Cooks

- Chefs

- Care assistants

- Drivers (non-LGV)

- Drivers (LGV)

- Commercial staff – see Procedure 0(I)8

ASSESSING APPLICANTS

This procedure deals with managing cash held for DBS checks

In this section:

- **Assessing your applicants**
- **Scoring the assessment**

|||||||||||||||||||||||||||||||||||||||||||||||||||||||||||||||||||||||||||||||||||||||||||||||||||||||||||||||||||||||||||||||||||||||||||

1 Assessing your applicants

1.1 Assess applicants using these guidelines.

1.2 Write the score on the application form in the space provided.

Appearance (App)

- Poor - Sloppy in dress, scruffy

- Average - Fairly neat and clean. Made some attempt at interview preparation

- Good -Neat, tidy, clean, well turned out

Attitude (Att)

- Poor - Aggressive, impatient, rude

- Average - Pleasant but not relaxed. May respond badly under pressure

- Good - Pleasant, friendly, polite, keen, relaxed, enthusiastic

Intelligence (Int)

- Poor - No formal qualification. Very poor handwriting

- Average - Basic qualifications. Legible handwriting

- Good - Good qualifications. Articulate. Neat writing. Could do written reports

Physique (Phy)

- Poor - Slow, frail and not very mobile

- Average - Fairly fit and mobile

- Good - Strong, quick and mobile

Hygiene (Hyg)

- Poor - Dirty, unwashed, unshaven and odour problem

- Average - Fairly clean but could do better

- Good - Clean, well groomed, tidy

2 Scoring your assessment

2.1 Add up the score. The maximum possible score is 15.

2.2 Do not use applicants scoring less than 10.

DAY SHEET

This procedure deals with managing cash held for DBS checks

In this section:

- ■ **Assessing your applicants**
- ■ **Scoring the assessment**

||||||||||||||||||||||||||||||||||||||||||||||||||||||||||||||||||||||||||||||||||||||||||||||||||||||||||||||||||||||||||||||||

1 Preparing a day sheet

1.1 Prepare day sheet using large piece of paper.

1.2 Draw columns.

1.3 Head columns with names of most frequently used grades of staff, for example waiting staff or LGV driver etc.

1.4 Use furthest right column for 'notes'.

1.5 Check through advance orders, extract those for the next day and record on day sheet under job grade.

1.6 On the sheet, note:

- Client name
- Job requirement, for example 1 x Kitchen porter
- Job start time, finish time, duration

1.7 Check through all orders for current week including completed orders and record requirement on day sheet as above.

1.8 Contact current and prospective customers and solicit orders for staff from them

1.9 Record on work order and then day sheet as above.

2 Load planning

2.1 Use day sheet for load planning.

2.2 On Fridays, write following week's orders onto job analysis sheet and dispatch from the job analysis.

2.3 Draw up day sheet but leave blank ready for Monday morning.

2.4 Retain day sheet for one week and then dispose.

Documentation

- Day sheet

VER: 1 26/04/2013

LOAD PLANNING AND MATCHING

This procedure deals with managing cash held for DBS checks

In this section:

- **Assessing your applicants**
- **Scoring the assessment**

|||||||||||||||||||||||||||||||||||||||||||||||||||||||||||||||||||||||||||||||||||||||||||||||||||||||||||||

1 Matching applicants to jobs

1.1 Looking through available staff application cards and select the person who best matches the customer's requirements in terms of:

- Has been specifically requested by the customer.

- Has previously successfully completed the assignment (Check 'performance' column of work history).

Otherwise select an applicant based on:

- Skill – Someone with the technical ability and knowledge to meet the requirements of the job description.

- Experience

- Qualifications

- Location – Someone who can easily reach the customer and speedily and cheaply (ie When travelling, does not have to cross too many zones)

- Availability – the applicant must be available for the full duration of the assignment.

- Personality – their personality fits the customers requirement.

1. 2 Pencil their name on the day sheet next to the particular job.

2 Unfilled orders

2.1 Contact other branches to borrow staff if there are requirements that might be difficult to fill.

Documentation

- Application card – See Resource 2a) (Page...)
- Day Sheet

DISPATCH

This procedure deals with managing cash held for DBS checks

In this section:

- ■ Assessing your applicants
- ■ Scoring the assessment

||||||||||||||||||||||||||||||||||||||||||||||||||||||||||||||||||||||||||||||||||||||||||||||||||||||||||

1 Briefing applicants for work

1.1 Load plan using day sheet to determine best-fit of workers with assignments. (See 0 (F) 3)

1.2 When the worker telephones, ask them to report to office for pre-assignment briefing.

1.3 If worker doesn't phone, call them.

1.4 Brief worker on:

- Details of assignment – job title, duties job description
- Start time, finish time, likely duration
- Customer details and travel instructions
- Whether agency or temporary
- Pay rate
- Prepare time sheet and issue to worker
- Confirm deadline for receipt of completed time sheets – 5.30 pm Friday.

1.5 NB Ensure that worker is fully briefed regarding duration of customer's assignment. Do not supply worker unless they can commit to duration of assignment.

1.6 Write worker's name, in pen, on the day sheet.

1.7 Place application card in 'out-working' box.

1.8 Telephone customer and confirm the name of their worker.

2 Unplaced workers

2.1 Write the name of any worker who telephones but does not get an assignment on the day sheet at the bottom of the relevant job title column.

Documentation

- Day sheet

WRITE UP

This procedure deals with managing cash held for DBS checks

In this section:

- **Assessing your applicants**
- **Scoring the assessment**

||||||||||||||||||||||||||||||||||||||||||||||||||||||||||||||||||||||||||||||||||||||||||||||||||||||||||||||

1 Recording the job details

1.1 Telephone customer and confirm if the worker has arrived on site. Do this **5-10 minutes** after the worker's scheduled start time.

1.2 Place tick against worker's name on day sheet.

1.3 From **day sheet,** record on job analysis:

- Worker's name
- Date
- Job
- Company

1.4 From **job analysis**, record on work order:

- Job
- Worker's name
- Invoice number
- Tick appropriate box of work history

1.5 From **work order**, record on job analysis:

1.6 From **job analysis**, record on application card:

- Date
- Customer name
- Job title
- Invoice number
- Tick appropriate box of work history

1.7 From **application card**, record on job analysis:

- P number

1.8 From **application card**, record on work order:

- P number

1.9 From **index card,** record on job analysis:

- Account number
- Rate code

1.10 Attach work order to application card(s) with paper clip.

2 Additional records

2.1 Complete job analysis and other work orders and application cards.

2.2 Prepare count sheet.

2.3 Place clipped work orders and application cards in 'out working' box.

2.4 Cross out entry on day sheet when write up has been done.

Documentation

- Day sheet
- Job analysis

- Work order

- Application card

- Index card

- Count sheet

COUNT SHEETS

This procedure deals with managing cash held for DBS checks

In this section:

- **Assessing your applicants**
- **Scoring the assessment**

||||||||||||||||||||||||||||||||||||||||||||||||||||||||||||||||||||||||||||||||||||||||||||||||||||||||||||||||||||||||||||||||||||||||||||

1 Compiling a count sheet

1.1 Compile a count sheet as soon as the staff for the day are checked in and written up.

1.2 Draw up a sheet of paper and head with the week-ending date, which is always Friday.

1.3 Draw columns for each grade of staff eg Kitchen porters, catering assistants or chefs etc.

2 Completing the count sheet

2.1 Go through the work orders and record each person day on the count sheet. Use gates ie

- If someone is **borrowed** from another branch, mark the count sheet but also include the number of people borrowed in a separate section.

- If a person is **lent** to another branch, record this separately. **DO NOT** include these workers in your total.

2.2 Total the figures to produce a daily count.

2.3 At the end of the week, use the count sheet to compile statistics.

2.4 File the count sheet in date order with the week's work orders.

Documentation

- Count sheet

VER: 1 26/04/2013

PERFORMANCE CONTROL CARDS

This procedure deals with managing cash held for DBS checks

In this section:

- **Assessing your applicants**
- **Scoring the assessment**

||||||||||||||||||||||||||||||||||||||||||||||||||||||||||||||||||||||||||||||||||||||||||||||||||||||||||||||||||||||||

1 Sending customers a performance control card

1.1 Send a card to a customer:

- The first time a customer uses a worker irrespective of the length of the assignment.

- After the first full week of any worker on any assignment.

- Once a month if the worker is in a long-term booking

- The first worker a customer has when they have not used for a month or more.

- In accordance with customer requirements.

1.2 Complete the relevant details on the card and send it to the customer with a reply paid envelope. Mark the two-digit service centre prefix and the branch name on the envelope.

2 Processing returned cards

2.1 Check the comments and mark the scores when a card is returned:

- 0 - for a tick in the 'poor' column

- 1 - for a tick in the 'average' column

- 2 - for a tick in the 'good'

2.2 Record the total score in the 'perf' (performance) column of the application card.

2.3 Staple the performance control card to the application form.

2.4 Speak to workers who receive a score of less than 12 about their performance.

2.5 Congratulate workers who receive a score of 16 (perfect).

Documentation

- Performance control card

CLIENT HISTORY CARDS

This procedure deals with managing client history cards

In this section:

- **Starting client history cards**
- **Completing client history cards**
- **Analysing client history cards**

||||||||||||||||||||||||||||||||||||||||||||||||||||||||||||||||||||||||||||||||||||||||||||||||||||||||||||||||||||||||||||||||||||||||||||

1 Starting client history cards

1.1 Create a yellow client history card for each client or unit as soon as they start using the service.

1.2 Complete all information neatly, legibly and accurately.

1.3 Obtain accurate information from customer as required.

1.4 Pay attention to obtaining full and accurate details regarding the customer, at least:

- Registered company name

- Registered address

- Invoice address

- Trading status - ie limited company, partnership or otherwise.

- Chief executive details

- Telephone and extension numbers

- Full contact names, including titles, first and last names

1.5 Take a client history card on the first service visit to make sure all the required information is collected.

1.6 Ensure that first service visit is made within one week of first order by a sales executive. If a sales executive is unavailable, ensure that a team leader visits.

1.7 Use the first visit to:

- Confirm and clarify information

- Confirm satisfaction with service

- Identify additional opportunities

- Obtain commitment to buy again

1.8 File cards in alphabetical order by company name.

1.9 In the case of catering contractors, councils or clients covering several units, create a control card.

2 Completing client history cards

2.1 Complete the usage section of the card every week from work orders.

2.2 Use calendar weeks.

2.3 Record usage as man days – one person for five days is five person days, two people for five days each is 10 person days, etc.

2.4 'Irr' stands for irritation. Irritations cover no shows, walk offs, poor performance, open or unfilled orders, lateness or any other instance of client dissatisfaction irrespective of whether or not the client complains.

2.5 On the control cards, maintain a running record of number of clients units using workers.

2.6 Establish visit programs to ensure that each client is visited at least once every six months.

2.7 Complete the reverse of the card with information drawn from visits. A client visit should always result in additional information being added to the card.

3 Analysing client control cards

3.1 Analyse cards every week to identify:

- Patterns of usage

- Seasonal influences on business levels

- Increases or falls in business whether gradual or sudden

- Business opportunities to increase or extend service provision

- Links between irritations and decline in business levels.

- Clients who have stopped using Care to Call

3.2 Visit each client who has had an irritation to discuss, resolve and obtain commitment to using again. Ensure visit takes place within 1 week of irritation occurring.

3.3 Visit any client whose usage declines to discuss, identify reason, resolve if service related and obtain commitment to re-establishing usage. Ensure visit takes place within 2 weeks of decline occurring.

3.4 Visit any client whose usage stops, especially where usage has been heavy to discuss, identify reasons, resolve and obtain commitment to re-establishing usage. Ensure visit takes place within 1 week of business ceasing.

3.5 Analyse control cards to identify general trends in usage.

3.6 When analysing cards, do not just look for problems and be satisfied if nothing is found. Assume that there is a problem and don't be satisfied until you find it.

3.7 As a last resort, if a client does not use for 26 weeks, transfer the details to a sales card and pass to sales department for follow up.

3.8 Ensure that all visit and operations options are exhausted before passing to sales.

Documentation

- Client History Card

COMPLAINTS

This procedure deals with managing complaints

In this section:

- **Receiving complaints**
- **Dealing with complaints**
- **Complaining to head office**

||||||||||||||||||||||||||||||||||||||||||||||||||||||||||||||||||||||||||||||||||||||||||||||||||||||||||||||||||||||||||||||||||||||||||||||||||

1 Receiving complaints

1.1 Customers, applicants, temporary workers, clients or others may complain if the service they receive does not meet their expectations.

1.2 Complaints should be welcomed as they illustrate weaknesses in the service and provide opportunities to review processes and implement improvements.

1.3 Complaints may be made:

- Verbally in the office

- Face to face; e.g. on client visits

- By telephone

- In writing, either to the local branch or direct to Head Office

1.4 A complaint is defined as:"Any instance of dissatisfaction expressed by a customer, applicant, temporary worker or others; where they wish that dissatisfaction to be regarded as a complaint".

1.5 Minor complaints can usually be resolved quickly with an apology and by making improvements. Nevertheless, still respond within one hour of receipt.

1.6 More serious or formal complaints will require a full investigation.

1.7 A more serious complaint is defined as:

- Any situation that involves the company in losing money, such as a reduced charge, at cost, no charge or otherwise concessionary invoice charge

- Any complaint received in writing

- Any formal complaint made over the telephone

- Any formal complaint where the complainant wishes to speak to 'the person in charge' or similar request

2 Dealing with complaints

2.1 The process for dealing with complaints is as follows:

- Acknowledge receipt in writing within one hour for a telephone/email complaint; and within three days for a written complaint

- Make sure that you understand the facts of the complaint (If the complaint is being made verbally, do not interrupt)

- Apologise

- Investigate the circumstances and speak to all the parties involved

- Do not reach conclusions in advance of the facts

- Give the complainant a response, setting out the relevant facts

- If restitution is needed, like a credit note, ensure this is issued speedily

- If the complaint is not upheld, then make sure that the complainant is informed

- Follow up complaints from clients to ensure that they are satisfied with the outcome

2.2 Record the details and the outcome of the complaint on a customer complaint form and retain a copy in a complaint file in the branch.

2.3 Each branch should have one complaint file, unless the branch has contracts which specifically require an individual complaint file.

VER: 1 26/04/2013

2.4 If an individual cannot resolve the complaint, or if further action is required, then the complaint form must be completed with details of the complaint and the action taken so far and then passed to the appropriate person.

2.5 Anyone receiving a complaint is responsible for informing the next most senior person.

3 Complaining to head office

3.1 Anyone who wishes to complain to the Care On Call head office should be advised to contact:

Care On Call
Address
Telephone:

3.2 An acknowledgment of the complaint will be sent, the complaint investigated, and a reply sent within 28 days.

3.3 District managers will be responsible for auditing complaint files every quarter and for ensuring steps are taken to prevent similar complaints arising.

PROCEDURE: O(S)1

STATISTICS AND PLANNING REVIEW

This procedure deals with compiling branch statistics

In this section:

■ **Managing statistics**

||||||||||||||||||||||||||||||||||||||||||||||||||||||||||||||||||||||||||||||||||||||||||||||||||||||||||||||||||||||||||||||||||||||||||||||||

1 Managing statistics

1 Prepare statistics in duplicate each week.

1.2 Record data honestly and accurately.

1.3 Refer to source documents to compile data:

- Advertising – use advertising record book

- Recruitment – use registration book

1.4 Production:

- People out, borrowed, lent – use count sheet

- Hours, NPO – use job analysis

- Clients, no-show, walk-off, poor performance, replaced, open orders, person days lost, cancelled order – use work orders

- New accounts – use account number register

1.5 Analyse data to identify trends, reveal problems, draw conclusions.

1.6 In conjunction with team leader, plan following week's activity using current week's statistics, for example:

- Advertising – recruitment needs and improving cost effectiveness. Use unit cost as the measure of effectiveness.

- Ideas to improve the conversion rate of responses to interviews

- Improving the quality of workers. Use NPM ratio as the measure of effectiveness.

- Ideas to increase the numbers of staff working and to reduce open orders and other indicators of poor performance etc

1.7 Implement ideas.

1.8 Prepare statistics the following week.

1.9 Compare achievement against plan to determine success of ideas.

1.10 Implement ideas.

1.11 Repeat cycle for process of continuous improvement.

1.12 Send copy of statistics to the area or district manager as required.

1.13 File original in branch in week order.

Documentation

- Statistics

ISSUING PERSONAL (P) NUMBERS

This procedure deals with personal (P) number procedures

In this section:

- **Managing personal (P) numbers**

||||||||||||||||||||||||||||||||||||||||||||||||||||||||||||||||||||||||||||||||||||||||||||||||||||||||||||||||||||||||||||||||||||||

1 Issuing a Personal (P) number

1.1 Ensure applicant has completed blue slip with:

- Name
- Address
- National insurance number
- Marital status
- Bank or building society account details

1.2 In 'P number' file, on next available entry line, record:

- Surname
- First names
- Date of first job
- National insurance number

1.3 If applicant has no National Insurance number, either record the date of the letter from the Benefits Agency saying the applicant has applied for a number, or the date of the applicant's appointment to get one.

1.4 Take the next P number in sequence

VER: 1 26/04/2013

1.5 Record that P number in the space provided on blue slip. Put slip in payroll drawer for submission to accounts department.

1.6 Record P number on a colour sticker and stick on application card, covering registration number.

Documentation

- Coloured sticker P number slip
- P number record file

VER: 1 26/04/2013

PROCEDURE: 0(P)2

ISSUING CLIENT ACCOUNT NUMBERS

This procedure deals with client account numbers

In this section:

■ **Managing client account nunbers**

|||||||||||||||||||||||||||||||||||||||||||||||||||||||||||||||||||||||||||||||||||||||||||||||||||||||||||||||||||||||||||||||||

1 Managing client account numbers

1.1 In 'account number' file, on next available entry line, record:

- Client name
- Contractor (if appropriate)
- Address
- First order date
- Type of order

1.2 Complete yellow new account slip with:

- Client name (including Ltd or PLC)
- Contractor (if appropriate)
- Full address including postcode and telephone number.
- Full invoice address including postcode (if different from above)
- Unit number (if appropriate)
- Type of account (eg net or gross in the case of catering contractors)
- Account number

1.3 Put slip in payroll drawer for submission to accounts department

VER: 1 26/04/2013

1.4 Record seven digit account number on yellow sticker and stick on index card in space provided.

1.5 If account subsequently changes (e.g. from gross to net or Level 2 terms to Level 1 terms) complete 'Client Account Transfer' form with relevant details and send to accounts department.

Documentation

- Account number record file
- Yellow new account slip
- Client/account transfer

PAYROLL PREPARATION

This procedure deals with time sheets and payroll

In this section:

- ■ **Issuing time sheets**
- ■ **Payroll and job analysis**
- ■ **Time sheets from earlier weeks**
- ■ **Post-processing procedure**

IIIIIIIIIIIIIIIIIIIIIIIIIIIIIIIIIIIIIIIIIIIIIIIIIIIIIIIIIIIIIIIIIIIIIIIIIIIIIIIIIIIIIIIIIIIIIIIIIIIIIIII

1 Issuing time sheets

1.1 Ask worker to report to the office for their pre-assignment briefing.

1.2 Issue them with a time sheet. Record:

- • Name
- • P number
- • Date Start
- • Job
- • Company
- • Travel details

1.3 Workers on assignment for more than one day who are cannot come to a pre-assignment briefing, must collect a time sheet from the office during the week.

1.4 Workers on assignment for only one day who cannot come to a pre-assignment briefing, must collect a time sheet form the customer.

1.5 Tell workers that the deadline for receiving a time sheet is 5:30pm Friday.

VER: 1 26/04/2013

2 Payroll and job analysis

2.1 Prepare the job analysis during write up. The job analysis is pre-printed with invoice numbers.

- Ensure that these are sequential.

- Use correct prefix for the service centre.

- Complete job analysis daily.

- Complete cross-references daily.

2.2 Collect coloured Personal (P) number forms and put in P number order.

2.3 Attach tax forms to P numbers forms.

2.4 Collect yellow new account forms and any other payroll forms, eg P45 requests, food hygiene deduction forms etc.

2.5 On job analysis, in 'notes' column, write 'new temp' and/or 'new client' as appropriate.

2.6 Sort time sheets into alphabetical order by worker surname. Process time sheets on a daily basis as they are received.

2.7 Look at the first entry on the first page of the job analysis. Find the correct time sheet. Check that time sheet details, like worker name, date, job, and customer, etc, tally with job analysis details.

2.8 Use a blue or black pen. Write neatly and clearly. Ensure numbers are legible.

2.9 From the time sheet; record on the job analysis:

- Time sheet number

- Total hours worked. If worker was lent, record half the total hours.

2.10 **NB** Use a ruler on the job analysis to ensure data is recorded or the correct line.

2.11 From the job analysis, record on the time sheet:

- P number

- Invoice number

- Cross reference number (if shown)

- Date including year (if not already recorded)

- Job (if not already recorded)

- Company (if not already recorded)

- Account number

- Purchase order number (if required)

- Rate code

2.12 On the time sheet:

- Check hours as shown in boxes to ensure that additions are correct

- Check that total number of hours is correct

- Check that time sheet is signed. If unsigned, do not process. Contact worker and inform them they must submit a signed time sheet

- Carry hours down into relevant boxes for basic pay, shift allowance, overtime etc. Refer to index cards for details.

- Carry total hours across into right hand column.

2.13 Separate top two white copies from green copy and place face down in separate piles.

2.14 If there is no green copy, or if information is recorded on a piece of headed paper, then:

- Prepare a new time sheet using the information provided

- In client's signature write: 'Reference your memo signed by ...

2.15 Fold the piece of paper, ensuring that the customer's signature is visible and staple to the back of the top two copies of the new time sheet.

2.16 Process the rest of the time sheets in the same manner.

3 Time sheets from earlier weeks

3.1 If the time sheet is dated earlier than the current week:

- Find the relevant entry in the carried forward book. Record the total hours worked and the day's date in the carried forward book.

- Use the file of previous week's job analyses to find the time sheet and complete the time sheet as 2.11 and 2.12 above.

- Write at the top of the time sheet 'Previous week'.

3.2 If there is more than one time sheet for the same job, but with differing dates in the same week:

- If there is a green copy but no white copies, proceed as 2.14 above.

- If rates shown on the job analysis are Pay X or Charge Y

- Then record on the time sheet accordingly.

3.3 **NB** Pay and charge rates may only be used in exceptional circumstances where rates cannot be drawn from the rate schedule. Such rates must be authorised by a district manager or above.

3.4 If hours are totalled incorrectly, telephone the customer to confirm correct addition.

4 Post-processing procedure

4.1 When all time sheets have been processed:

- Sort time sheets into P number order. While sorting, check for mistakes – e.g. missing data, incorrect additions, etc.

- Use 'payroll checklist' as a guide

- Clip together all time sheets for the same worker, using a paper clip

4.2 Total up the days worked by each worker (not the total number of assignments) up to a maximum of five.

4.3 Find the worker's orange and record the number of days worked, for example:

- Worker has worked 1 day record 1

- Worker has worked 2 days record 2

- Worker has worked 3 days record 3

- Worker has worked 4 days record 4

- Worker has worked 5 days record 5

- Worker has worked 6 days record 5

VER: 1 26/04/2013

- Worker has worked seven days record five

4.4 **NB** It does not matter which days have been worked. Include Saturday and Sunday, but never record more than five.

4.5 Clip the orange slip to the front of the time sheets **DO NOT** staple.

4.6 Use separate orange slips for carried forward time sheets and record the number of days worked accordingly. Attach tax documents to the front of time sheets using a paper clip

4.7 Attach blue slips to front of time sheets using a paper clip

4.8 Put all time sheets with blue slips and/or tax forms attached, together.

4.9 Put all time sheets without blue slips and/or tax forms attached, together.

4.10 Put additional documents eg yellow new account slips or invoices etc, together.

4.11 Separate the two copies of the job analysis.

4.12 Put all documents and the job analysis top copy in a large envelope.

4.12 Write on the envelope:

- Branch
- Service Centre
- Two digit prefix

4.13 Ensure envelope reaches accounts department by 9 am Tuesday.

Documentation

- Time sheet
- Job analysis
- Blue P number slip
- Tax forms
- Yellow account number slip
- Payroll guide

- Index card
- Carried forward book
- Orange day's worked slip

SUPPLEMENTARY TIME SHEETS

This procedure deals with supplementary time sheets

In this section:

- **Managing supplementary time sheets**

||||||||||||||||||||||||||||||||||||||||||||||||||||||||||||||||||||||||||||||||||||||||||||||||||||||||

1 Supplementary time sheets

1.1 Use supplementary time sheets to correct underpayments and under-charges generally caused by using incorrect rate codes or mistakes in adding up.

1.1 As soon as an error is identified, telephone the customer to explain the situation.

1.2 Find original green copy of the time sheet.

1.3 On <u>new</u> time sheet, write:

- Worker's name

- P number

- A <u>new</u> invoice number – **DO NOT** use invoice number from original time sheet

- Use date from <u>original</u> time sheet

- Job, department, company account number as per original time sheet

- Correct rate code or the addition being charged e.g. '£0.50p'

- Total hours to be charged

- Customer details as per original

- In main body of time sheet, write: "Supplementary to invoice number

<invocie number>. Original invoice charged at £10 per hour – correct charge is £10.50. Charge x hours at 50p." Or a similar short, clear explanation of the reason

1.4 If worker requires payment, write details on lower section of time sheet.

1.5 In client's signature, write: "As per original time sheet <time sheet number> as attached to <invoice number>.

1.6 Obtain authorisation from district or area manager.

1.7 Send top two copies to accounts with payroll.

1.8 File the green copy. Staple the yellow copy to original green copy to which the supplementary time sheet refers

1.9 Record details of supplementary in credit note/supplementary book. Record:

- Worker's name
- Invoice number
- Original invoice number
- Company
- Hours & amount
- Reason

Documentation

- Time sheet – see Resource 3 (Page 178)
- Credit note – see Resource 4 (Page179)
- Supplementary book.

CREDIT NOTES

This procedure deals with credit notes

In this section:

- **■ Issuing a credit note**

IIIIIIIIIIIIIIIIIIIIIIIIIIIIIIIIIIIIIIIIIIIIIIIIIIIIIIIIIIIIIIIIIIIIIIIIIIIIIIIIIIIIIIIIIIIIIIIIIIIIIIIIIIIIIII

1 Issuing a credit note

1.1 Use credit notes to correct mistakes in invoicing usually caused by the use of incorrect rate codes, mistakes in adding up, or using incorrect account numbers

1.2 Prepare credit notes **as soon as mistakes are identified.** Where a credit note is requested by a customer, check the original invoice fully to ensure that a credit not **is** actually due.

1.3 Find the original green copy.

1.4 Take a blank time sheet and with **red ink**, write:

- Worker's name

- Personal (P) number

- A new invoice number from the current week's job analysis

- In reference number, write the invoice number of the original invoice

- The date of the **original** invoice

- Job – as original

- Company – as original

- Account number – as original

- Rate – as original

1.5 In the upper hours section of the time sheet, write: "Credit note ref invoice <invoice number>. Company overcharged by <number of hours> hours", or a similar short, simple, clear explanation of the reason.

1.6 Write the number of hours credited in the hours box.

1.7 NB If the worker has been overpaid, write a deduction slip and attach to one of their other time sheets. Deductions from pay **<u>cannot</u>** be made from credit

1.8 Obtain authorisation from area or district manager.

1.9 Send top two copies to accounts. File the green copy. Staple the yellow copy to original green copy to which credit not refers.

1.10 Complete job analysis in red ink. In 'notes' column, write: "Credit note. Ref invoice <invoice number>, the number of hours and value"

1.11 Record details of credit note in credit note/supplementary book. Record:

- Worker's name
- Invoice number
- Original invoice number
- Company
- Hours and amount
- Reason

Documentation

- Time sheet – Resource 3 (Page 178)
- Credit note – Resource 4 (Page 179)
- Supplementary book.

RE-RAISING INVOICES

This procedure deals with post-credit note processes

In this section:

■ **Re-raising invoices**

‖‖

1 Re-raising an invoice

1.1 Use re-raises to correct invoices following a credit note. (See 0 (P) 8)

1.2 Process re-raises at the same time as a credit note is prepared.

1.3 Take a blank time sheet and using **blue or black ink,** write:

- Workers name

- Personal (P) number

- A **NEW** invoice number from the current week's job analysis

- In reference number, write the invoice number of the original invoice

- The date of the original time sheet

- Job – as original time sheet

- Company – as original time sheet

- Account number – for the correct client to be invoiced

- Rate – for the relevant job

1.4 In the upper hours section of the time sheet, write a short explanation for the re-raise, for example, the wrong client was charged on the original invoice.

1.5 Write the number of hours to be re-raised in the hours box.

1.6 Obtain authorisation from operations manager.

1.7 Send top two white copies to accounts along with the top two white copies of the credit note.

1.8 File green copy. Staple yellow copy to original green copy to which re-raise refers.

1.9 Complete job analysis in blue or black ink. In "notes" column, write "re-raise".

TEMPORARY TO PERMANENT

This procedure deals with temporary staff taken on as permanent works by clients

In this section:

- How temporary to permanent works
- Temporary to permanent fees
- Confirming a temporary to permanent switch

||||||||||||||||||||||||||||||||||||||||||||||||||||||||||||||||||||||||||||||||||||||||||||||||||||||||||||||||||

1 How temporary to permanent works

1.1 Temporary to permanent allows a temporary worker to be hired permanently by a customer.

1.2 This is only available for temporary workers who are already working for a customer. Do not sell to customers as a cheap way of hiring a permanent member staff.

2 Temporary to permanent fees

2.1 Charges are generally - but not always - based on a descending scale over 10 weeks. For example:

- Worker taken on by customer after less than 1 week - £1000

- Worker taken on by customer after 1 week - £900

- Worker taken on by customer after 2 weeks - £800

- Worker taken on by customer after 3 weeks - £700

- Worker taken on by customer after 4 weeks - £600

- Worker taken on by customer after 5 weeks - £500

- Worker taken on by customer after 6 weeks - £400

VER: 1 26/04/2013

- Worker taken on by customer after 7 weeks - £300

- Worker taken on by customer after 8 weeks - £200

- Worker taken on by customer after 9 weeks - £100

- Worker taken on by customer after 10 weeks - Free

3 Confirming a temporary to permanent switch

3.1 There is **NO** guarantee **WITH TEMPORARY TO PERMANENT**.

3.2 The customer uses the period of temporary work to determine the worker's suitability.

3.3 If the worker subsequently leaves or is dismissed, **NO REFUND IS PAYABLE TO THE CUSTOMER.**

3.4 Agree with the customer when the worker is to join their payroll and confirm the charge payable.

3.5 Inform them that there is no guarantee and the fee is non-refundable. Record the details of who you spoke to in the 'notes' column of the job analysis.

3.6 Raise an invoice on the job analysis.

3.7 On a blank time sheet, record:

- Worker's name

- Personal (P) number

- Invoice number

- Date

- Job title

- Customer name

- Account number

3.8 In the upper hours section, write:

"Temporary to permanent charge re <worker's name> in accordance with our standard charges. Confirmed with <customer name and job title> by

<your name> on <date>.

3.10 Complete a temporary to permanent letter template letter .

3.11 Send time sheet and letter in payroll to ?

3.12 With some customers, temporary to permanent charges are **NOT** applied. Ensure that this is recorded on index cards.

Documentation

- Timesheet – See Resource 3 (Page 178)
- Temp to Perm Template Letter.

VER: 1 26/04/2013

PAID LEAVE

This procedure deals with paid leave entitlement and procedures

In this section:

- ■ **Paid leave entitlement**
- ■ **Managing claims for paid leave**

1 Paid leave entitlement

1.1 Ensure that hired applicants read and sign the terms of engagement at interview.

1.2 Issue them with the Welcome to Care On Call booklet.

1.3 Explain that they are entitled to paid leave once they start work, providing the gap between assignments is no more than 12 weeks in a row.

1.4 Someone who does not work for more than 12 consecutive weeks has to re-register and start paid leave qualification again.

1.5 The paid leave entitlement after qualification is one day for every 8.28 days worked (Monday to Friday) up to a maximum of 28 days a year backdated to the when they started work with Care On Call

1.6 Complete 'work history' to track paid leave entitlement as the worker is booked on assignments.

1.7 Apart from work details, like the date, job, customer and invoice numbers, record the financial week number.

1.8 In the Days of Week (DofW) box, insert the total number of days worked in the week, but not the number of separate assignment days.

1.9 Exclude Saturday and Sunday unless the worker works them as part of an ongoing shift pattern. Also exclude bank holidays unless the worker works them.

1.10 Insert a running total of days worked in Days to Date (DtD) box. For example:

Week 32

DofW	5
DtD	5
HT	5

Week 33

DofW	4
DtD	9
HT	5

1.11 When a work history is completed, insert 'days to date' in carried forward box.

1.12 Staple a second work history to application card.

1.13 On the new work history insert days to date in the brought forward box.

1.14 At the end of a year, which is the last Friday in the year, carry forward any balance of ? or more days.

1.15 The leave year is the calendar year.

1.16 Once qualified, leave is earned in the period January to the end of the following December.

1.17 Leave may be taken up to the end of March of the following year.

2 Managing claims for paid leave

2.1 A worker must request paid leave. It is not paid automatically.

2.2 When they request leave, issue them a 'paid leave request' form. NB A worker must visit the office to complete the form. DO NOT post to them.

2.3 A worker who fails to request their leave within 12 weeks of stopping work loses the leave.

2.4 Ensure that the worker fills in their own name, branch. personal (P) number, number of days claimed and the dates they intend to take leave.

2.5 Check the dates claimed and ensure that request forms are not processed before leave is taken. Payment is due after leave has been taken.

2.6 Check their entitlement by looking at their work history. Look at the last 'days to date' entry.

2.7 Divide by 8.28 to find their paid leave entitlement. **NB** Only use complete sets of 8.28 days. For example:

- 8 days worked – entitlement is nil as the days worked total less than 8.28

- 10 days worked - entitlement 1 day as 10 includes one set of 8.28 days

2.8 Complete the office use section of the paid leave request form with:

A) Days to date
B) Entitlement (A divided by 8.28)
C) Deduct any days taken
D) Days due (B – C)

2.9 Enter the days claimed in the days claimed box.

2.10 Write your name and the date and pass to a supervisor to check and authorise.

2.11 Complete a time sheet with the number of days to be paid.

2.12 Attach claim form to time sheet as authorisation. Insert invoice number on claim form. Use 'holiday pay' account number.

2.13 On work history, record leave payments as:

- Financial week number

- Date

- In customer, write "John Smith"

- In job, write "holiday pay"

- Invoice number

- In HT (holiday taken) box, insert number of days processed

2.14 Highlight all entries.

2.15 When determining future leave entitlements, deduct any holiday days taken from the year to date entitlement.

2.16 Leave for one year that has not been taken by 31 March of the following year is lost.

2.17 Payment in lieu of leave not taken is illegal.

PAYMENT IN LIEU

This procedure deals with payments in lieu to staff

In this section:

- **Payment in lieu entitlement**
- **Making payment in lieu**

1 Payment in lieu entitlement

1.1 Payment in lieu of holiday is only payable when:

- A worker has completed an assignment in each of 12 weeks.

- They have had, or requested, a P45

- Paid leave is requested within 12 weeks of their last assignment.

1.2 Check requests for payment in lieu for compliance with each of the conditions in Section 1.1 above.

2 Making payment in lieu

2.1 If the conditions in Paragraph 1.1 are met, check the worker's holiday entitlement and process according to Procedure 0(P)10.

2.2 On the worker's work history, in addition to other information required, write:

- The amount paid in lieu

- P45 issued

2.3 Cross out Personal P number

2.4 File and application card.

Documentation

- Terms of Engagement – Resource 2c
- Welcome to Care On Call booklet – Resource 2d
- Application card with work history – Resource 2a
- Paid leave request form
- Timesheet – Resource 3

PAYING TEMPORARY WORKERS (BACS)

This procedure deals with paying temporary staff

In this section:

- **Setting up payment by BACS**
- **BACS payments and payslips**

||||||||||||||||||||||||||||||||||||||||||||||||||||||||||||||||||||||||||||||||||||||||||||||||||||||||||||||||||||

1 Setting up payment by BACS

1.1 Temporary workers are paid through the Bank Automated Clearing Service (BACS), direct into their bank or building society account.

1.2 There is no facility to pay workers by any other method.

1.3 Ask all applicants to bring details of their account when they come for an interview.

1.4 Under no circumstances may applicants use someone else's bank account to get paid.

1.5 Processing or attempting to process temporary staff pay through the bank account of a permanent staff member is regarded as gross misconduct, liable to summary dismissal.

1.6 Each applicant must complete a blue payroll information slip at interview.

1.7 The information required is:

- Name, address, date of birth, marital status and national insurance number

- Bank or building society account details

- Declaration by worker

1.8 **DO NOT** complete the information for the applicant - they must do this themselves.

1.9 **NB** Information should be known or apparent to the worker from their cheque book or other documentation. If it is not obvious, and the applicant is unsure, tell them to check with their bank. **DO NOT GUESS**.

1.10 Check that the applicant has written the information clearly and that they have not made mistakes like putting the wrong date of birth, or too many digits in their bank account number.

1.11 Bank account information is "sensitive" personal data under the Data Protection Act and must remain confidential. Do not let any unauthorised person see the data. Bank account forms must be destroyed by shredding.

2 BACS payments and payslips

2.1 When a worker is sent to their first job, create a Personal (P) number (see O (P) 1), complete the shaded area, remove the slip from the application card and place in the payroll drawer.

2.2 Send the blue slip to accounts with the worker's first time sheet.

2.3 BACS payments are normally made on Wednesday and normally arrive in bank account on a Friday.

2.4 Depending on the type of account, money should be available over the counter from cash machines on the same day.

2.5 Pay slips are normally available for collection from head office on Wednesday evening.

2.6 Workers should collect their payslip from the branch. Ask the worker to sign against their name on the list provided.

2.7 **NB**: Some pay days are subject to change due to public holidays.

2.8 When all pay slips are collected, return the top copy of the list to accounts and file the bottom copy in the branch.

2.9 Issue a **green 'change of account' form** to workers who wish to change their bank or building society account details.

2.10 Applicants who leave and subsequently return must complete a new bank details form.

2.11 If money goes astray because the worker gives incorrect details, the company is not be liable. Recovery of money in these circumstances is at the discretion of the bank.

Documentation

- Blue payroll information slip and payment details
- Green change of account slip
- Payslip signing sheet

TAX

This procedure deals how income tax works

In this section:

- **Introduction to income tax**
- **Workers who do not pay tax**
- **How tax works**
- **Tax-free pay explained**
- **What is basic rate tax?**
- **Tax codes and forms**
- **Some common tax terms**

|||||||||||||||||||||||||||||||||||||||||||||||||||||||||||||||||||||||||||||||||||||||||||||||||||||||||||||||||||||||||||||

1 Introduction to income tax

1.1 Ask if the applicant has a P45 at interview.

1.2 Give the applicant a P46 if they do not have P45.

1.3 Submit the P45 or P46 with first time sheet.

1.4 Provide information and guidance to temporary workers based on the following notes. If the following notes do not address their queries, refer them to the tax office.

1.4 Most temporary staff, with few exceptions, pay income tax on their earnings.

1.5 A staff controller is responsible for giving applicants help and advice about their tax. All staff are expected to familiarise themselves with current tax information.

1.6 Do not under any circumstances, provide applicants with inaccurate information, so do not give an answer without checking the facts first.

2 Workers who do not pay tax

2.1 The only workers who need not pay tax are:

- Students in full time education during recognised holidays

- Certain individuals who operate as a company and invoice for work that they perform, like surveyors.

2.2 These, however, must be cleared with the accounts department first.

3 How tax works

3.1 Most people will be entitled to tax free pay. They will then pay income tax on the remainder of their income.

3.2 **NB** Tax is due on gross earnings - that is the amount before deducting National Insurance Contributions.

3.1 Tax will be deducted by the accounts department through the PAYE system. This stands for "Pay as you Earn" and means that tax will be deducted and then if an individual is entitled to a rebate (return of tax), they will receive the money at a later date.

3.4 The only exception to this is a person's first full time job since leaving full-time education, where the tax office is awaiting their code.

4 Tax-free pay explained

4.1 Unless a person is on "basic rate", everyone is entitled to a certain amount of income in the course of a tax year without paying tax. This tax-free pay will vary according to an individual's circumstances.

4.2 Note that tax free pay has nothing to do with the amount that is earned.

4.3 Someone may claim allowances if they are a single parent with a child under 16, make pension contributions or incur certain expenses in their work.

4.4 The most common reasons for decreasing a person's tax free pay are:

- Owing back tax.

- Having a company car.

5 What is basic rate tax?

5.1 After tax free pay, a person pays income tax on the remainder of their income at the basic rate.

5.2 Tax free pay is only available in one job, so an applicant who has a full time job but works for Care On Call on their days off will pay basic rate on all their earnings through us.

6 Tax codes and forms

6.1 They produce a tax code after investigating an individual's circumstances. Tax records are computerised but the tax office still relies on some tax forms, the most common of which are:

Form P45

A P45 ise issued to everyone leaving full-time employment and shows their earnings in the tax year in that job, tax paid and tax code on leaving.

A P45 is a valuable document and duplicates cannot be provided.

The P45 will only show an NI number if the employer knew the employee's NI umber was.

A P45 does not mean a person pays less tax but that they will pay the correct tax.

Form P46

Must be completed by all applicants if they cannot provide a P45. A P46 puts an applicant on emergency tax if they do not have another job. If the applicant has another job, they will be put on basic rate.

Form P38(S)

Completed by students in full-time education. A P38(S) lets a student to have their pay tax-free, but only during recognised holidays.

A student must complete a P38(S) every time they work during holidays.
Form P60

Available to applicants (provided when requested) who are employed in the penultimate and last week of the tax year, which shows earnings and tax paid during the year. Workers who leave at other times in the year must request a P45.

Form P6

An instruction from the tax office to an employer to put an applicant on a specific tax code. Applicants normally receive a copy of the cosing fro their tax office. Anyone with queries about their coding should contact their tax office.

7 Other common income tax terms

7.1 Here are some answers to frequently asked questions about income tax:

What is emergency or 'week one' tax?

Emergency or 'week one' tax means that, although someone receives tax free pay, each week of the tax year is treated as if it was the first, so tax-free pay is not cumulative.

What does 'cumulative' mean?

This means that you can earn tax-free pay each week. For temporary staff earning different amounts over a number of weeks, cumulative tax is often the best option. Cumulative tax status is indicated on a tax code that does not include the letter X, like 615L.

What if someone has a tax complaint?

Don't forget that Care On Call is not responsible for making tax rules, only complying with them. If someone does not understand or believe a response to a tax query, they should speak to their tax office.

PROCEDURE: 0(G)1

LAWS AFFECTING AGENCY OPERATIONS

This procedure deals how income tax works

In this section:

- Introduction to income tax
- Workers who do not pay tax
- How tax works
- Tax-free pay explained
- What is basic rate tax?
- Tax codes and forms
- Some common tax terms

|||||||||||||||||||||||||||||||||||||||||||||||||||||||||||||||||||||||||||||||||||||||||||||||||||||||||||||||||||||||||||||||||||

1 Introduction to employment law

1.1 Relevant legislation may be broadly divided into three categories:-

Laws promoting good conduct of employment agencies

- Employment Agencies Act

- Nursing Agencies Act

Legislation affecting specific types of employment

- Health and safety legislation

- Road traffic laws

General laws affecting employment

- Terms and conditions of employment

- Pay and taxation

- Trade descriptions and advertising

- Sex discrimination

- Racial discrimination

- Employment of foreign workers

- Disability discrimination

1.2 Most legislation is drafted by the government in the isolation of their own departments and requirements. Only a small part of general legislation is relevant to employment agencies. Much is conflicting and does not cater for the unique situation of temporary staff.

1.3 A tremendous number of complex rules amended by successive new laws renders comprehensive analysis beyond the scope of this manual.

1.4 The manual presents only an outline of the most common laws and how they apply to Care On Call operations.

2 Law and agency conduct

2.1 Applying the rules depends on the type of organisation the agency is -

- An employment agency is an organisation supplying permanent employees

- An employment business is an organisation supplying temporary employees

- A nursing agency supplies qualified nursing staff. Unqualified staff are supplied by an employment agency or business

3 Law and agency operations

3.1 Under current legislation and case law, an employment business or nursing agency are not regarded as employers.

3.2 If this were not so, a business like Care On Call could not operate, for example, legal obligations towards temporary staff could not be fulfilled and employing HGV drivers would be illegal without an operator's licence and the fleet of vehicles needed to support a licence application.

3.3 As a business, Care On Call could not manage every worker in every work place.

3.4 For nursing agencies, the expertise required by staff and managers and the number of mandatory obligations and procedures, are so specific that the client acceptance of the employer's role may be taken for granted. Furthermore, as licensing by the local authority concerned is dependent on health authority advice, the conduct of the agency is indirectly governed by the client.

3.5 In the case of an employment business, 'grey areas' which may tempt some clients to evade their legal obligations while holding Care On Call responsible for their subsequent problems.

3.6 Although a case like this is unlikely to succeed before the courts, the publicity could be costly and detrimental to the corporate image.

3.7 Although Care On Call operates as an agency and a business, the company only operates as an agency. All "temps" are technically 'permanent staff on short-term contract and should be referred to as "contract staff".

3.8 While mandatory legislation for conditions of employment fall to the client, this is not intended as a means that lets Care On Call evade any moral obligations of good service, high standards of care and fair treatment to clients and applicants.

3.9 As an agency, Care On Call is bound by legislation concerned with:-

- Nursing Agency Conduct
- Employment Agency Conduct
- Pay and Taxation
- Trade Descriptions
- Sex Discrimination
- Racial Discrimination
- Employment of Foreign Nationals
- Disability Discrimination

3.10 The staff highlighted must understand and observe the following legal requirements.

4 Nursing Agencies (Managers and Medical Supervisors)

4.1 The selection of qualified applicants must take place under the supervision of a registered and qualified nurse or medical practitioner. Non-qualified staff must interview under supervision and must have sufficient experience and training to understand all client and applicant requirements.

4.2 Interview, records and the checking of applicant information must be strictly in accordance with Care On Call procedures.

4.3 Premises must be maintained to a "'reasonable' level.

4.4 Contract staff gross profit margins (commission) are based on a percentage of the cost. This is contract staff gross pay including premium rates, excluding National Insurance Contributions. and VAT.

4.5 The upper limit may be set by the licensing authority and is expressed as a percentage of cost of sales, which is the pay plus the fee.

4.6 Rates of pay generally cannot exceed those laid down by the Whitley Scale, although this may vary between health service trusts.

4.7 The Call On Care licence number must appear on all correspondence, literature and invoices

4.8 VAT is only applied to commissions.

5 Employment Agencies (Managers and Operational Staff)

5.1 Personal information about the client and applicant must be adequate for proper referral and must remain confidential.

5.2 Qualifications or permits required by law for specific occupations must be checked.

5.3 Fees may not be charged to applicants nor inducements given to them to leave their job.

5.4 Advertising for applicants need not reveal the identity of the agency but must make clear that the advert is on behalf of an agency.

5.5 Terms and conditions of supply and fee scale must be sent in writing and on receipt of order to:-

- New clients
- Old clients re-ordering after conditions and fees have been amended.

5.6 Anyone under 18 cannot be employed without confirmation of vocational guidance by an education authority careers officer.

5.7 Young persons may be sent for employment abroad but the requirement are such that Care On Call will not participate in such contracts or placements.

5.8 Adult contracts or placements abroad, other than for a UK based employee, will not be made without director's permission. Directors should consult Statutory Instrument 1976 no. 715, part II, para 6.

5.9 Records must be kept and retained in accordance with Care On Call procedures.

6 Pay & Taxation (All Staff)

6.1 Pay and tax rules are applied to contract staff for employers and subsequently recovered from them with Care On Call fees.

6.2 In accepting this task, Care On Call accepts responsibility for obtaining all applicant information, making statutory deductions and remitting any deducted together with returns required under income tax employment regulations.

6.3 Operational staff should obtain the information detailed in Care On Call procedures from applicants. Accounts staff will calculate taxes, make and remit deductions and deliver returns as laid down in the current Employers Guide to PAYE issued by HM Revenue and Customs.

6.4 Contract staff must be paid for their work as soon as possible after completion. This includes providing a payslip detailing the method of gross pay calculation, the amount of taxes deducted and any other information affecting the net amount.

7 Trade Descriptions (Managers and Operational Staff)

7.1 Care On Call operating ethics render this section superfluous. It is included merely to remind staff that advertising will:-

- Be based on actual requirements

- Express the true facts

- Not distort or embellish facts and figures to increase their attraction

7.2 The above determines the responsibility of all order takers to obtain adequate and accurate information.

8 Sex Discrimination (Managers and Operational Staff)

8.1 Discrimination can arise in matters concerning either pay or terms and conditions of employment, can apply to either gender. In both cases, discrimination may be broadly defined as unfavourable treatment of one gender compared with the other.

8.2 Pay is covered by the Equal Pay Act 1970, and employment by the Equality Act 2010. The latter applies also to discrimination by reason of marital status.

8.3 While Care On Call is not the employer of contract staff nor of persons recruited for permanent jobs, it is unlawful to aid or assist in sex discrimination. Care On Call cannot therefore knowingly be a party to such action by an employer.

8.4 However, if information taken from an employer in good faith, subsequently leads to unforeseen and unwilling discrimination, Care On Call cannot be held responsible.

8.5 The above paragraphs apply equally to applicant advertising and recruitment where terms offered and selection may not include sex as discriminatory criteria.

8.6 Furthermore, in advertising, it is unlawful to use descriptions like "waiter" or "salesgirl" that has gender connotations unless the advertisement clearly indicates that discrimination is not intended.

8.7 Sex discrimination is not unlawful in employment where a person's gender is a genuine occupational qualification (GOQ).

8.8 GOQs are concerned mainly with issues like working at single-gender changing facilities or providing personal care services in a nursing home.

9 Racial Discrimination (Managers and Operations Staff)

9.1 The Equality Act 2010 defines discrimination as "direct" and "indirect".

9.2 Direct discrimination arises when someone treats another less favourably on racial grounds than they would treat someone else.

9.3 Indirect discrimination is concerned with racial groups and the inability of the majority of the group to comply with unjustified conditions, imposed on racial grounds, like the qualification for receiving a benefit sought by an individual.

9.4 Discrimination can be applied to a variety of things but as far as Care On Call is concerned, it simply means that it will not be practised – directly or indirectly – on grounds of colour, race nationality or origin, in relation to:

- Recruitment
- Selection
- Dispatch
- Terms offered

9.5 Nor will Care On Call assist others by accepting or filling orders conditional on racial discrimination, unless racial characteristics constitute a GOQ.

9.6 An agency cannot be held responsible for subsequent racial discrimination by an employer, to whom a person has been introduced in good faith nor if the employer has quoted a reasonable GOQ. exception which the agency has accepted in good faith.

9.7 In cases where discrimination appears permissible as in any concerning race, record all instructions received.

10 Employment of Foreign Nationals (Managers and Operations Staff)

10.1 The rules are completed by the exceptions. However, most of them are outside the scope of Care On Call operations and the following general principles apply.

10.2 Workers from European Union countries are permitted to look for and take work without a permit.

VER: 1 26/04/2013

10.3 Subject to certain exceptions, all other workers from overseas, subject to immigration control, require permits.

10.4 Permits are only issued for certain types of work providing the vacancy cannot be filled by someone from Great Britain or the European Union.

10.5 Permits may only be sought by and issued to the intending employer therefore CAN NOT BE OBTAINED BY CARE ON CALL.

10.6 All applicants for employment, IRRESPECTIVE OF N ATONALITY, must provide proof of entitlement to work in the UK.

10.7 This may be in the form of a national insurance number appearing on an official document, or a passport or birth certificate. (See O (I) 3 Nationality for full details).

11 Disability Discrimination

11.1 Discrimination on grounds of an applicant's disability is unlawful unless it can be shown to be justified.

11.2 A disabled person is defined as anyone with a physical or mental impairment that has a 'substantial' and 'long-term' negative effect on their ability to do normal daily activities.

11.3 Reasonable adjustments must be made to accommodate an applicants disability.

11.4 These adjustments must be made if an employer should reasonably have known that someone was disabled.

11.5 Employment agencies (even though not the employer of temporary staff) are covered by legislation and must not discriminate or assist an employer to discriminate against the temporary staff.

VER: 1 26/04/2013

Appendices

Examples of Disclosure levels and examples of relevant posts
Guidance for Disclosure Applicants
Terms of Engagement with equal opportunities CRB statement.
Code of Practice
Table of identity documents and how to check for authenticity.
Guidance on completing of Disclosure Application forms
Category codes
Guidance for Counter-Signatories on completing Sections W, X, Y.
Disclosure application continuation sheet.
Policy statement – Secure storage, handling, use, retention, and disposal of Disclosures and Disclosure information.

APPENDIX A

1 Disclosure and Barring Service Disclosures

1.1 The Disclosure and Barring Service (DBS) offers two levels of disclosure depending on the contact an applicant might have with children and vulnerable adults during the course of their duties.

2 DBS Enhanced Disclosure

2.1 DBS enhanced disclosure covers posts which involve a significant contact with children or vulnerable adults.

2.2 Workers needing an enhanced disclosure include:

- Support workers
- Nursery nurses
- Social workers
- Domiciliary care workers
- Escorts for school children
- Bus or taxi drivers regularly transporting children or vulnerable adults

2.3 Enhanced disclosure includes a police records check to discover if the applicant has any convictions or cautions that might prevent them working with children or vulnerable adults and confirmation if they are the subject of any criminal investigation.

2.4 The disclosure is sent under separate cover to the employer, but not to the applicant, and **MUST NOT** be revealed to the applicant.

2.5 It will also include a Independent Safeguarding Authority Register check which details comments from employers about any risk the applicant might pose to children or vulnerable adults.

2.6 Where disclosure is needed, clients will generally require the enhanced level, which is the Care On Call default disclosure application.

3 DBS standard disclosure

3.1 The standard disclosure is primarily for posts that involve working with

VER: 1 26/04/2013

children or include regular contact with vulnerable adults.

3.2 Workers needing an standard disclosure include:

- Nurses (who do not specifically work with children)

- School ancillary staff e.g. caretaker, catering staff, bursar who do not have regular access to children.

- Taxi drivers (with no specific remit to transport children or vulnerable adults).

3.3 The disclosure covers details of all convictions and cautions held by the police, including current and 'spent' convictions as well as details of any cautions, reprimands or final warnings.

3.4 The disclosure includes a check against the Independent Safeguarding Authority Register.

APPENDIX B

1 Applicant's Guide to the Disclosure and Barring Service

1.1 The Disclosure and Barring Service (DBS), an executive agency of the Home Office, gives access to criminal records and other information to organisations in England and Wales through a service called disclosure.

1.2 The aim is to help organisations make better informed decisions when recruiting people into positions of trust.

1.3 The DBS service is available to professional, licensing and regulatory bodies whose volunteers, employees and licensees are not necessarily in direct contact with children and vulnerable adults, but still need to uphold the highest standards of professional performance.

1.4 Disclosure can help improve these recruitment decisions.

1.5 Through the DBS service, organisations can provide greater protection for the vulnerable members of society and afford greater protection to their customers, staff, volunteers and, ultimately, their organisation.

2 What information is available through disclosure?

2.1 The DBS provides access to different types of information, such as:

- Details on the Police National Computer (PNC), such as convictions, cautions, reprimands and warnings in England, Wales and those recorded from Scotland. Some Northern Ireland conviction data is also held on the PNC.

- Details by local police relating to relevant non-conviction information

- Information from the Independent Safeguarding Authority register

3 Levels of disclosure

3.1 To provide this service, DBS offers two levels of disclosure, each representing a different level of check. The two levels of disclosure are standard and enhanced.

3.2 These disclosures cannot be obtained by the public and are only available to organisations for those professions, offices, employments, work and occupations listed in the Exceptions Order to the Rehabilitation of Offenders Act 1974.

VER: 1 26/04/2013

3.3 Care On Call only acknowledges the enhanced disclosure.

4 Enhanced disclosure

4.1 Enclosed disclosure is for posts involving a far greater degree of contact with children or vulnerable adults. In general, the type of work will involve regularly caring for, supervising, training or being in sole charge of such people.

4.2 Examples include a teacher or scout leader. Enhanced disclosures are issued for some statutory purposes, such as gaming and lottery licences.

4.3 Enhanced disclosure contain the same information as standard disclosures, plus any information held on local police files about the applicant

5 Why might I be asked to apply for a disclosure?

5.1 You might have been asked to apply for a disclosure if you will be working:

- With children vulnerable adults

- In an establishment that is wholly or mainly for children; in healthcare

or

- Have applied to be a foster carer, adoptive parent or childminder.

5.2 A disclosure may also be required for a range of other types of job or licences.

5.3 To find out more please contact the DBS information line on 0870 909 0811 or visit the DBS website at https://www.gov.uk/government/organisations/disclosure-and-barring-service/about

6 I have a disclosure from another company. Can I use it again?

6.1 No. A disclosure is not transferable between companies.

7 What if I have lived overseas?

7.1 If you lived overseas, applying for a disclosure may not be worthwhile, as the DBS does not generally have access to overseas criminal records.

7.2 However, some organisations have a legal responsibility to check if a person is banned from working with children or vulnerable adults and can only do this through the DBS.

7.3 The DBS can also advise on how to obtain equivalent information from the overseas authorities. You may wish to discuss this with your prospective employer.

8 How do I apply for a disclosure?

8.1 You will be asked to:

- Complete an application form handed to you by the person who asked you to apply.

- Prove your name, address and date of birth, along with the registered body name and number, and the level of disclosure required. This will help the person who asked you to apply to confirm your identity. A guidance leaflet on how to complete the form will be provided.

9 Who will receive my disclosure?

9.1 When the application is processed, the DBS sends a copy of the disclosure containing any information revealed during the search, to you and the person who countersigned your form.

10 Will information in my disclosure stay confidential?

10.1 Organisations using the DBS must comply with the DBS Code of Practice, which is there to make sure the whole process works fairly and that any information revealed is treated fairly and securely. Also, the DBS is committed to compliance with the Data Protection Act. This means that any personal information that you submit to us will be protected.

10.2 Under the code, sensitive personal information must be handled and stored appropriately and must be kept for only as long as it is necessary.

10.3 The code is published on the DBS website, or you can request a copy from the person who asked you to apply for the disclosure.

11 What if I have a criminal record that is irrelevant to the job application?

11.1 Safeguards and guidelines have been introduced to ensure conviction information is not misused and that ex-offenders are not treated unfairly.

11.2 Ex-offenders will retain the protection afforded by the Rehabilitation of

Offenders Act 1974. In addition, the DBS and the Chartered Institute of Personnel and Development (CIPD) have developed guidance information for employers on this matter.

12 What if things go wrong?

12.1 The DBS has established a comprehensive complaints process and as part of our commitment to provide a high standard of customer service will always:

- Act fairly and impartially

- Communicate effectively

- Deal promptly with all enquiries

- Try to learn from our mistakes

13 How long are disclosures valid?

13.1 Each disclosure will show the date of printing. Disclosures do not carry a predetermined period of validity because a conviction or other matter could be recorded against the subject of the disclosure any time after issue. Expiry dates will depend on the organisation you are applying through.

APPENDIX C

1 TERMS OF ENGAGEMENT – AGENCY AND TEMPORARY WORKERS

1.1 In this document, the following definitions apply:

- 'Company' means Care On Call trading

- 'Hirer' means the person, firm or corporate body using the services of a worker supplied by the company

- 'Worker' means a work-seeker as defined by regulations

- 'Regulations' means The Conduct of Employment Agencies and Employment Businesses Regulations 2003

1.2 The company is an employment business as defined by the regulations.

1.3 Work is offered to you on the basis of a contract for services with the company. You do not have to accept any assignment offered to you and the company makes no guarantee as to the number of assignments which may be offered to you, if any. For the avoidance of doubt, you do not have contract of service and are not considered as an employee of either the company or any hirer for whom you may work. There is no contractual relationship between you, the company or the hirer, if you are not working.

1.4 An assignment will last for a maximum of one week. If your services are requested for a following week, you will be offered a new assignment. One assignment shall not be regarded as continuous with another. If you wish to end an assignment you should inform the hirer and the company at the end of a day's work. You are not required to give notice. Either the company or the hirer may end an assignment at any time by informing you at the end of a day's work.

1.5 The company does not charge a fee for work-finding services. Where the company offers other services (eg training courses) for which a fee is charged, you are not obliged to use the company but may source the service from other providers. Any assignment offered is not dependent on you using any of the company's other services.

1.6 The company will seek work for you commensurate with your experience, qualifications, training and authorisation to work. You undertake to inform the company if your situation should change (eg a qualification expires) and you are therefore no longer eligible to work in a position.

VER: 1 26/04/2013

The company does not pay less than the minimum wage. The actual rate of pay for any assignment will be confirmed when you are offered the assignment. The company agrees to pay you for work done even if the company does not get paid by the hirer. You undertake to fulfil your duties to the best of your ability and not to behave in ways which might prevent the hirer paying the company. Pay is subject to statutory deductions and is weekly in arrears via BACS credit transfer to a bank account which must be in your own name. The company does not pay by any other method.

1.7 The Working Time Regulations 1998 restrict working hours to an average of 48 hours in a week. 'Working time' is time spent working on assignment and excludes travelling time or breaks. You may choose to work more than 48 hours. If you regularly work at least three hours between midnight and 7am you are a night worker and must undergo a health assessment. This will be provided free of charge.

1.8 You are entitled to paid leave at the rate of one day for every 8.28 days worked up to a maximum of 28 days a year. Leave is earned in the calendar year January 1 to December 31. All leave must be taken by March 31 of the following year. Leave may not be carried forward. There will be no payment in lieu.

1.9 Pay is the average basic hourly rate multiplied by the average hours worked per day to a maximum of the preceding 12 weeks. Holiday pay when you cease work providing you have requested a P45 and no more than 12 weeks has elapsed since completing the last assignment. If no assignments are undertaken for more than 12 consecutive weeks, these terms of engagement lapse and you must re-register with the company.

1.10 The company's terms with hirers entitle the company to recompense if you are offered employment with the hirer either directly or through another employment business or employment agency.

1.11 No variation or alteration of these terms of engagement shall be valid unless the details of such variation are agreed between a director of the company and you, and set out in writing with a copy of the varied terms given to you stating the date on or after which the varied terms apply.

1.12 You consent to the company sharing relevant information about you (including, but not limited to, references and copies of certificates or qualifications) with hirers for the purposes of assisting you in seeking work.

1.13 **I agree to these terms and have received a copy. I confirm that all**

information provided in support of my application is true, and any documents provided are legal, genuine and authentic.

Signed:

_____

Name:

_____

Date:

_____

If you do not ever wish to work more than 48hrs in a week, sign here:

_____

2 DISCLOSURE AND BARRING SERVICE

2.1 Care on Call is committed to the fair treatment of its staff, potential staff or users of its service, regardless of race, gender, religion, sexual orientation responsibility for dependants, age, physical/mental disability or offending background that does not create risk to children and vulnerable adults.

2.2 As an organisation using the Disclosure and Barring Service (DBS) to assess applicants' suitability for positions of trust, Care On Call complies fully with the DBS Code of Practice and undertakes to treat all applicants for positions fairly. We undertake not to discriminate unfairly against any subject of a disclosure on the basis of conviction or other information revealed.

2.3 We actively promote equality of opportunity for all with the right mix of talent, skills, and potential and welcome application from a wide range of candidates, including those with criminal records. We select all candidates based on their skills, qualification and experience.

2.4 A disclosure is only requested after a thorough risk assessment has indicated that one is proportionate and relevant to the position concerned or is a requirement of working, we encourage all applicants to provide details of their criminal record early in the application process.

VER: 1 26/04/2013

2.5 We ensure that all those involved in the recruitment process are suitably trained to identify and assess the relevance and circumstances of offences. We also ensure that they have had appropriate guidance and training in the relevant legislation relating to the employment of ex-offenders.

2.6 At interview, or subsequently, we ensure that an open and measured discussion takes place on the subject of any offences or other matter that might be relevant to the position. Failure to reveal information that is directly relevant to the position sought could lead to withdrawal of an offer of work.

2.7 The DBS has produced a Code of Practice which you may see on request

2.8 We undertake to discuss any matter revealed in a disclosure with you.

2.9 Having a criminal record will not necessarily bar someone from working for us. That will depend on the circumstances.

2.10 Please read and answer the following declaration and then sign where indicated.

Have you ever been convicted, cautioned, reprimanded or given a warning by the police for any reason including motoring or juvenile offences?

Yes ☐　　No ☐

If yes, please give details:

_____

_____

_____

_____

_____

2.11 NB You may work in positions that are covered by the Rehabilitation of Offenders Act 1974 (Exceptions) (Amendment) Order 1986 which means that all convictions cautions, reprimands and warnings on your criminal record need to be disclosed. You must also disclose any current or pending police action against you.

2.12 Applicants are advised that if they have been banned from working with people under the age of 18, or if they appear on the Protection of Children Act list or the Protection of Vulnerable Adults list, it is a criminal offence to <u>seek </u>such work.

2.13 Information you provide will be kept confidential except where it is relevant to an application for work. Put the details here:

_____

_____

_____

3 DECLARATION

3.1 The information I have provided is to the best of my knowledge true and correct. If appropriate to my work, I agree to apply for a DBS disclosure and pay the appropriate fee. I agree to inform Care On Call if the DBS contact me in any form before, during or after the disclosure application process. I also agree to inform Care On Call of any future police action which may be taken against me and/or if I am referred to the Protection of Vulnerable Adults or Protections of Children Act lists.

Signature:

_____

Print Name:

_____

Date:

_____

VER: 1 26/04/2013

Appendix D

1 DISCLOSURE AND BARRING SERVICE CODE OF PRACTICE

1.1 This code of practice is published under section 122 of the Police Act 1997 ("the Act") in connection with the use of information provided to registered persons ("disclosure information") under Part V of that Act.

1.2 Disclosure information is information:

- Contained in criminal record certificates under section 113 of the Act (which are referred to in this code as "Standard disclosures")

- Contained in enhanced criminal record certificates under section 115 of the Act (referred to in this code as "Enhanced disclosures")

- Provided by the police under section 115(8) of the Act

1.3 Except where indicated otherwise, the code of practice applies to all recipients of disclosure information – that is to say:

- Registered persons

- Those countersigning disclosure applications for registered persons

- Others receiving such information

1.4 Where reference is made to "employers", this should be read as including any person at whose request a registered person has countersigned an application, including:

- Voluntary organisations and others engaging, or using the services of, volunteers

- Regulatory and licensing bodies

1.5 Further information in relation to the code, and other matters relating to registered persons and others having an involvement with disclosure information, is contained in an explanatory guide.

2 OBLIGATIONS OF THE CODE

2.1 These are as follows:

Fair use of disclosure information

2.2 Recipients of disclosure information shall:

- Observe guidance issued or supported by the Disclosure and Barring Service ("the DBS") on the use of disclosure information – and, in particular, recipients of disclosure information shall not unfairly discriminate against the subject of disclosure information on the basis of conviction or other details revealed

2.3 In the interest of the proper use of disclosure information and for the reassurance of persons who are the subject of disclosure information, registered persons shall:

- Have a written policy on the recruitment of ex-offenders, so that a copy can be given to all applicants for positions where a disclosure will be requested

- Ensure that a body or individual at whose request applications for disclosures are countersigned has such a written policy and, if necessary, provide a model for that body or individual to use

2.4 In order that persons who are, or who may be, the subject of disclosure information are made aware of the use of such information, and be reassured employers shall:

- Ensure that application forms for positions where disclosure will be requested contain a statement that a disclosure will be requested in the event of a successful application, so that applicants are aware of the situation

- Include in application forms or accompanying material a statement to the effect that a criminal record will not necessarily be a bar to obtaining a position, in order to reassure applicants that disclosure information will not be used unfairly

- Discuss any matters revealed in disclosure information with the person seeking the position before withdrawing an offer of employment

- Make every subject of a disclosure aware of the existence of this code of practice, and make a copy available on request; and in order to assist staff to make appropriate use of disclosure information in reaching decisions, make available guidance in relation to the employment and fair treatment of ex-offenders and to the Rehabilitation of Offenders Act 1974

Handling disclosure information

2.5 Recipients of disclosure information:

- Must ensure that disclosure information is not passed to persons not

VER: 1 26/04/2013

authorised to receive it under section 124 of the Act. Under section 124, unauthorised disclosure is an offence

- Must ensure that disclosure and the information they contain are available only to those who need to have access in the course of their duties

- Should retain neither disclosures nor a record of disclosure information contained within them for longer than is required for the particular purpose. In general, this should be no later than six months after the date on which recruitment or other relevant decisions have been taken, or after the date on which any dispute about the accuracy of the disclosure information has been resolved. This period should be exceeded only in very exceptional circumstances which justify retention for a longer period

2.6 Registered persons shall:

- Have a written security policy covering the correct handling and safekeeping of disclosure information

- Ensure that a body or individual at whose request applications for disclosures are countersigned has such a written policy, and, if necessary, provide a model for that body or individual to adopt.

Assurance

2.7 Registered persons shall:

- Co-operate with requests from the DBS to undertake assurance checks as to the proper use and safekeeping of disclosure information;

- Report to the DBS any suspected malpractice in relation to this code of practice or any suspected offences in relation to the misuse of disclosures.

Umbrella bodies

2.8 An umbrella body is one which has registered with the DBS on the basis that it will countersign applications on behalf of others who are not registered.

2.9 Umbrella bodies must satisfy themselves that those on whose behalf they intend to countersign applications are likely to ask exempted questions under the Exceptions Order to the Rehabilitation of Offenders Act 1974.

2.10 Umbrella bodies must take reasonable steps to ensure that those to

VER: 1 26/04/2013

whom they pass disclosure information observe the code of practice

Failure to comply with the code of practice

2.11 The DBS is empowered to refuse to issue a disclosure if it believes that a registered person; or someone on whose behalf a registered person has acted, has failed to comply with the code of practice

APPENDIX G

1 CATEGORY CODES

1.1 Enter a category code in Section Y of the application form which relates to the work the applicant will undertake.

1.2 Code 01 is the only code used. Other codes are for information only.

CATEGORY 1

Working in one of the following:

- An institution exclusively or mainly for the reception and treatment of children
- A hospital which is exclusively or mainly for the reception and treatment of children
- A care home, residential care home, nursing home or private hospital which is exclusively or mainly for children
- An educational institution
- A children's home or voluntary home
- A home **provided** under Section 82 (S) of The Children Act 1989

CATEGORY 2

- Working at day care premises

CATEGORY 3

- Caring for, training or being in sole charge of children

CATEGORY 4

- Caring for, training or being in sole charge of children

CATEGORY 5

- Caring for children under 16 in the course of their employment

CATEGORY 6

- Where a substantial part of normal duties includes supervising or training children under 16 in the course of their employment

CATEGORY 7

One of the following positions:

- Member of the governing body of an educational institution
- Member of a relevant local government body
- Director of social services of a local authority
- Chief education officer of a local education authority
- Member of the Youth Justice Board for England and Wales
- Children's Commissioner (or deputy) for Wales
- Members of the Children and Family Court Advisory and Support Service (CAFCASS)

For these purposes, a person belongs to a relevant local government body if:

- They are a local authority member or executive and discharge any education or social service functions of a local authority
- They are a member of an executive of a local authority which discharges any such functions
- They are a member of a committee of an executive of a local authority, an area committee or any other committee of a local authority which discharges any such function.

CATEGORY 8

Supervising or managing an individual in his work in a regulated position

CATEGORY 9

Working in a further education institution where the normal duties of that work involve regular contact with persons aged

CATEGORY 10

A vulnerable adult is a person aged 18 or over who receives services of a

VER: 1 26/04/2013

type listed in paragraph 1) below and in consequence of a condition of a condition of a type listed in paragraph 2) below, has a disability of a type listed at 3) below:

1. The services are:

   a. Accommodation and nursing or personal care in a care home

   b. Personal care or support to live independently in his or her own home

   c. Any services provided by an independent hospital, clinic, medical agency or National Health Service body

   d. Social care services

   e. Any services provided in an establishment catering for a person with learning difficulties

2. The conditions are:

   a. A learning or physical disability

   b. A physical or mental illness, chronic or otherwise including alcohol or drug addiction

   c. A reduction in physical or mental capacity.

3. The disabilities are:

   a. A dependency upon others in the performance of, or a requirement for assistance in the performance of, basic physical functions

   b. Severe impairment in the ability to communicate with others, or impairment in a person's ability to protect him or himself from assault, abuse or neglect.

VER: 1 26/04/2013

VER: 1 26/04/2013

APPENDIX H

COMPLETING DISCLOSURE APPLICATION FORM SECTIONS W, X AND Y

Form ref	Information required
58	**Evidence checker's name** Write in the name of the person who has seen the evidence and checked the applicant's details against their documents
59	**Once the true identity** has been verified from the applicant's documents against Sections A and B, complete the 'Yes' box
60	Complete the 'Yes' box
61	Fill in the position applied for with as much details as possible ie 'school catering assistant'
62	Write 'Care on Call' in this section
63	The criminal record check required for the application Put 'X' in the Enhanced box
64	**'Are you entitled to know whether this applicant is registered to work with children?'** Put 'X' in this box Any applicant subject to disclosure may work in a position that involves contact with children, therefore **ALL** applicants subject to disclosure must be checked against lists held by the Department of Health and Department for Education and Skills
65	**'Are you entitled to know whether this applicant is registered to work with vulnerable adults?'** Put 'X' in this box Any applicant subject to disclosure may work in a position that involves contact with vulnerable adults, therefore **ALL** applicants subject to disclosure must be checked against the Protection of Vulnerable Adults (POVA) scheme
66	**Does the position involve working with children or vulnerable adults at the applicant's home?** Complete the 'No' box
67	Put 'X' in the Yes box
68	**Registered body number.** Complete with the Care on Call number (1-47438820) if not already pre-printed in Section Y
69	Complete with your counter-signatory number. The number and signature at line 9 must belong to the same person

VER: 1 26/04/2013

Form ref	Information required
70	**Registered body to pay** Care on Call has a credit arrangement with the Disclosure and Barring Service (DBS). The '**On Account**' box will already have been completed by the DBS.
71	**Declaration by registered person** Read the declaration statement and sign in the box
72	**Date of countersignature** Enter the date when the form was completed and signed

NB: USE BLACK INK ONLY TO COMPLETE THE FORM

VER: 1 26/04/2013

Appendix J

To: Accounts Department

From: _____

Branch: _____

Date: _____

Number of DBS applications sent: _____

Amount of cash sent: £

Amount of cheques sent: £

Amount of Postal Orders sent: £

Total: £

NB: Do not take cash payment unless the applicant cannot pay by another method

How is payment sent (Tick box):

☐   Internal post delivered to Head Office by _____

☐   Internal post delivered by courier _____

☐   Other (Speciffy): _____

COMPLETE THIS FORM AND SEND SEPARATE FROM DBS APPLICATIONS

To: Accounts Department

DBS applicants and method of payment

Applicant name	Cash or cheque

VER: 1 26/04/2013

Appendix L

SECURE STORAGE, HANDLING, USE, RETENTION AND DISPOSAL OF DIS-CLOSURES AND DISCLOSURE INFORMATION

1 General Principles

1.1 As an organisation using the Disclosure and BArring Service (DBS) scheme to help assess the suitability of applicants for position of trust, Care On Call complies fully with the DBS Code of Practice regarding the correct handling, use, storage, retention and disposal of disclosures and disclosure information.

1.2 Care On Call complies fully with its obligations under the Data Protection Act and other relevant legislation pertaining to the face handling, use, storage, retention and disposal of disclosure information.

2 Storage and Access

2.1 Disclosure information is either kept in an applicant's personal file or in a separate file. Whichever is the case, information is kept securely in lockable, non-portable storage cabinets with access strictly controlled and limited to those who are entitled to see it as part of their duties.

2.2 Disclosures may be seen by inspectors from the Commission for Social Care Inspection or by others who are conducting inspection for the purposes of determining compliance with obligations.

3 Handling

3.1 In accordance with Section 124 of the Police Act 1997, disclosure information is only passed to those who are authorised to receive it in the course of their duties.

4 Usage

4.1 Disclosure information is only for the specific purpose for which it was requested and for which the applicant's full consent has been given.

5 Retention

5.1 Once a recruitment (or other relevant) decision has been made, we will not keep disclosure information for more than 12 months.

VER: 1 26/04/2013

6 Disposal

6.1 Once the retention period has elapsed, we will ensure that any disclosure information is suitably destroyed by secure means, ie by shredding, pulping or burning.

6.2 While awaiting destruction, disclosure information will not be kept in any insecure receptacle.

6.3 We will not keep any photocopy or other image of the disclosure or any copy or representation of the contents of a disclosure.

6.4 However, we may keep a record of the date of issue of a disclosure, the name of the subject, the type of disclosure requested, the position for which the disclosure was requested, the unique reference number of the disclosure and the details of the recruitment decision taken.

VER: 1 26/04/2013

Made in the USA
Charleston, SC
22 February 2016